Front cover: Adam in the Scottish Burgh: The 'New' Brig at Ayr, c. 1785, edited and built without his supervision (Strathclyde Regional Council)

Back cover: [...] north side Charlo[...] influenced the later ch[...] [...]own of Edinburgh. (National Trust for Scotland)

Frontispiece:
Robert Adam and Scotland:
traditional castle features at
Caldwell House, Ayrshire,
which he designed in 1773-4.
(Royal Commission on the
Ancient and Historical
Monuments of Scotland.
Photograph, Professor Alistair
Rowan)

SCOTTISH
RECORD OFFICE

ROBERT ADAM *and* SCOTLAND

Portrait *of an* Architect

Margaret H B Sanderson

EDINBURGH: HMSO

ACKNOWLEDGEMENTS

Thanks are due to Sir John Clerk of Penicuik, Bt, Mr Keith Adam of Blair Adam and the Trustees of the National Library of Scotland for permission to quote extensively from letters in the Clerk of Penicuik Muniments, the Blair Adam Muniments and the Paterson-Adam Correspondence; and to those private owners, galleries and other bodies who have given permission for manuscripts, portraits, drawings and photographs from their collections to be reproduced as illustrations. These are individually acknowledged throughout the book. Photographs of material held in the Scottish Record Office were taken in the photographic department of the National Library of Scotland. Engravings reproduced as the front cover and colour plate 4 were photographed by Mr Andrew M Broom, Deputy Keeper, Scottish Record Office. Colour plate 1 is from a photograph taken by Mr M Brookes. I am grateful to the Society of Architectural Historians of Great Britain and the Editor of *Architectural History* for permission to quote from the substance of my article on 'Robert Adam's last visit to Scotland, 1791', which appeared in Volume 25 of that Journal (1982).

Crown Copyright 1992
First printed 1992

ISBN 0 11 494205 6

INTRODUCTION

Robert Adam has paid the price of having made one of the most personal contributions to architectural art of all time; for many people he has become a 'style', mainly in interior decoration. Even his personal appearance is probably best recognised in the posthumous portrait medallion by James Tassie which at first glance may suggest a decorative item by that other eighteenth-century stylist, Josiah Wedgwood. He is associated with a firm of 'the Adam Brothers' and, having invested in an artistic education in Europe, is known to have joined the Scottish brain-drain to London where he gained the reputation that has made his name a household word.

This limited and impersonal popular image falls far short of the reality. Robert Adam's output of designs covered an enormous range of work: from whole buildings or their substantial remodelling, with their internal decoration and furnishings, to town-planning schemes, public works, bridges, monuments and garden buildings, and items for personal use ranging from a sedan-chair for the Queen to the title-page for a book by a friend.

The artist himself was a lively personality who could be both expansive and obsessive. The young Thomas Telford, the future engineer, job-hunting in London in 1782, found his fellow-countryman 'affable and communicative'. According to the family it was difficult to catch his expression in a portrait. They did not care for Tassie's attempt, which was done from a death-mask taken by Nollekens; '... it has something of the general air of the face,' Robert's sister Peggy decided, 'but the features are not like ... It is disagreeable to transmit an unjust resemblance of a great genius'.

The diversity of gifts within the Adam firm has become clearer in recent years thanks to the researches of architectural historians. Most welcome in this connection has been the emergence from the shadows of William Adam, early-eighteenth century Scotland's 'universal architect' and father of the Brothers, who has thereby not only gained his own rightful place but given to the firm the human face of a family.

It has also become clear that Robert Adam's relationship to Scotland has had to be re-assessed, his joining the brain-drain to the south notwithstanding. Like many expatriate Scots he had a lifelong love-hate relationship with his native country which had helped to mould him but on which he turned his back in his late twenties as 'a narrow place' where 'scarce will ever happen the opportunity of putting one noble thought in execution'. Even in the brilliantly successful 1760s he remained involved with the family firm, while the 1770s saw important and innovative work by him in Scotland. There followed a period of financial problems, frustration and a drop in creative output partly due to changing architectural fashion. Then in the last decade of his life many commissions came in from Scottish clients; it was an unexpected homecoming.

What is remarkable about the later years of his career is not only the energy which the ageing architect was able to summon in the face of this new challenge but the high level of creativity with which he fulfilled it. We have come to appreciate that the distinctive castles and restrained villas, the plans to transform the townscape of Scottish cities (largely unrealised) which he produced towards the end of his life must be taken as seriously in their way as part of his work as those spectacular commissions which he carried out in the early years of his London practice.

This present account attempts to put Robert Adam's work for Scottish clients, north and south of the Border, his relationship to the family firm and the inspiration which he drew from Scotland into the context of his wider career. In doing so it draws attention to the importance of the documentary sources of architectural history. Although surviving buildings and the architect's drawings (of which there are thousands from the Adam office) are of supreme importance in any study of his work, these are complemented and can often be interpreted by written sources of information on the building history of many of his commissions and the society for which they were created: accounts, building contracts and schedules, business letters and details of the activities of craftsmen of all kinds. Since, like other artists, he did not create in a vacuum private letters and other family papers can illuminate his ideas, contacts, experience and personality.

In particular, the book makes use of the variety of records held by the Scottish Record Office whose headquarters building, the General Register House, was purpose-designed by Robert Adam to hold the national archives of Scotland. It has been published as a tribute to the Architect in his Bicentenary year and for the information and enjoyment of all those who value the buildings that have been left to us by him and other members of the Adam family.

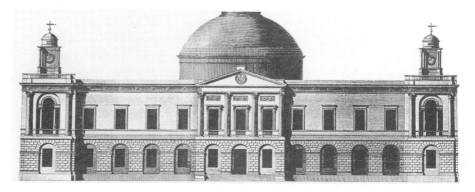

General Register House, Edinburgh. Robert Adam, 1771

CONTENTS

Part one

A NARROW PLACE

ARCHITECTS AND GENTLEMEN

The profession of architect came of age during the lifetimes of William Adam and his sons. The skill of designing a building as distinct from the practical knowledge required for its construction became formally recognised in 17th century Scotland with the use of the word 'architect', especially in the case of those officials responsible for the royal buildings. These were the Masters of Works, who controlled expenditure and the employment of craftsmen and labourers, and the Master Masons who were in charge of actual building operations on the site.

The first official to be called 'king's architect', actually on his tombstone, was William Shaw, appointed Master of Works in 1583, who came from a landed family but had a flair for designing castles and could at the same time draw up rules for practising masons. From a craft background came James Murray, a second-generation master wright, who became Master of Works in 1607 and was referred to as king's architect five years later. He is known to have designed the parliament hall in Edinburgh among other works. In 1612 he enhanced his social position by acquiring the lands of Kilbaberton where he may have designed his own house.

John Mylne (d.1667), architect of the Tron kirk, Edinburgh, who was descended from a line of royal Master Masons going back to the 15th century, is celebrated in an inscription as a man who combined the roles of royal architect and practical craftsman:

> 'Rare man he was, who could unite in one
> Highest and lowest occupation,
> To sit with Statesmen, Councillors and Kings
> To work with Tradesmen, in Mechanick Things'.

John's nephew, Robert Mylne (d.1710), who was also Master Mason to the crown, purchased estates in Fife and the Lothians with the profits of speculative building; he is commemorated in Edinburgh by Mylne's Court and Mylne's Square. His son Thomas (d.1763) built up a considerable architectural practice, purchased the estate of Powderhall near Edinburgh but remained a prominent figure in the mason craft; he was a founder member of the grand lodge of freemasons in Scotland. Thomas's sons were the contemporaries of Robert Adam and his brothers who pointedly referred to them as 'the sons of Deacon Mylne', accentuating their craft rather than professional connections. Master masons who were not royal officials were also found among the craftsmen-architects of the late seventeenth century. These included the active Tobias Bauchope, mason in Alloa, who in 1684 contracted with a landowner, Stirling of Herbertshire, to take down and rebuild the kirk of Logie 'conforme to ane draught [plan] drawen be the said Tobias himself'.

Bauchope worked as a builder for Sir William Bruce (1630-1710), a landed gentleman from outwith the craft tradition whose appearance on the architectural scene gave the profession an acceptable social standing in Restoration Scotland. Bruce's position and earlier political career (Jacobite though he was) made him the social equal of those gentlemen-amateurs who enjoyed architecture as an intellectual pursuit, collecting books on the subject for their libraries and sharing an enthusiasm for Antiquity in general and the historical origins of classical architecture in particular. Sir John Clerk of Penicuik (1676-1755), the doyen of the gentlemen-amateurs, called Bruce 'the introducer of Architecture into this country'. He meant, of course, classical architecture. Two of Bruce's finest houses are Kinross House which he designed for himself and Hopetoun House, which William Adam later remodelled on an even grander scale.

Scottish buildings in the native tradition were ingeniously-planned, well-built in stone and often exuberantly decorated inside. During the renaissance of the 16th and 17th centuries the design and decoration of buildings such as the royal palaces, the castles of the great landowners, the houses of prosperous merchants

Plans, elevation and garden layout for Kinross House, Kinross-shire, for Sir William Bruce. The drawing is attributed to Alexander Edward who was employed to make scale drawings from Bruce's sketches. c.1685. *(Royal Commission on the Ancient and Historical Monuments of Scotland)*

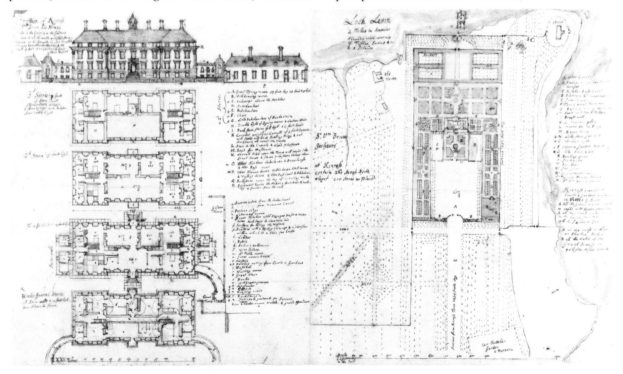

as well as churches and other public works had demonstrated the effects of Scotland's direct links with the intellectual and artistic life of Europe. The work of Sir William Bruce and the classical architects who followed him belongs to a period when influences tended to come through England where Scottish architects, amateur and professional, often made tours of country houses.

Bruce's successor in the office of Overseer of the Royal Works in Scotland was James Smith (c.1645-1731) who first appears in 1678 as a master mason under Bruce during the remodelling of Holyrood. He married a daughter of Robert Mylne, becoming a burgess of Edinburgh in her right, and bought the small estate of Whitehill near Musselburgh. About that time he was described as an 'architectour, a man who hes the repute to be very skilled in works of that nature'. Two other commentators described him, independently, as 'the most experienced architect in Scotland' and as 'having the best skill of them all'. Smith most closely followed the career of a professional architect with a list of fine country houses to his credit, a number of them designed for the lesser newly-established gentry to whom Smith and his fellow craft-trained architects came to belong. Associated with Smith in some of his work was Alexander McGill who was made architect to the burgh of Edinburgh in 1720. His own works included the main block of Mount Stuart (1718-22) for the 2nd Earl of Bute and the layout of a village near Edinburgh for the Picardy weavers (1730). John, 6th Earl of Mar (1675-1732) was the most skilled gentleman-amateur of the early 18th century. His schemes included the layout of grounds as well as houses. He spent much of his exile in Europe after the 1715 Jacobite Rising designing houses for English, Scottish and French owners, corresponding with James Gibbs (*see below*) and William Adam.

It was not long before the followers of the new profession took their talents out of Scotland in the tradition of Scots from other walks of life: merchants, soldiers, scholars and artists. Two of the most prominent in the early eighteenth century were Colen Campbell (1676-1729) and James Gibbs (1682-1754), both of whom had had alternative professional prospects before turning to architecture: the first in the law and the second in the Roman Catholic priesthood. Both had studied in Italy. That and the fact that they both settled and practised in London is an indication of their international outlook. This is also demonstrated in Campbell's influential book, *Vitruvius Brittanicus* in which the architectural plates (which included a number of his own works) formed an argument in favour of the style of the great sixteenth-century Italian master Palladio which Campbell was largely responsible for reviving in Britain. James Gibbs was a contemporary of the English architects Vanbrugh and Hawksmoor and surveyor of the fabric of Wren's London churches, his own best-known work in that city is probably the church of St Martin-in-the-Fields. He wrote several books on architecture to add to the growing reference library available to the eighteenth-century practising architect.

By the first quarter of the century not only was classical architecture flourishing in Scotland but Scots-born architects had begun to influence fashion outwith their own country.

The Parliament House, 1632–40; designed by James Murray of Kilbaberton, Master of Works

Layout for the improvement of the grounds around Alloa House, Clackmannanshire, by John 6th Earl of Mar, 1722-31. *(Register House Plans, 13258/3)*

*W*illiam Adam (1689-1748) belonged to the tradition of craftsmen-architects. His forebears, after holding land at Fanno in Angus in earlier centuries had by mid-seventeenth century become burgesses of Forfar where at least three generations can be found as master masons[1]. When the subject of ancestry arose in conversation in Italy in the 1750s Robert told his acquaintances, so he jokingly wrote to his family, that 'the Adams are of so old a family that from the days of our first father they have never been able to trace them and that the first of them I ever heard of was one Sir John Adam who had a cross erected to his memory at Forfar on account of his great actions in war and wise councils in peace – concealing like grim death that said Sir John was but the operator and head *cowan* [mason] of said cross. A good lie well timed sometimes does well'. William Adam's father, John, and two other Adams who are almost certainly his brothers were masons, a third was a baxter in Forfar whose son, Mr Patrick Adam merchant in Kingston, Jamaica, made William his executor in his will in 1747. The mason craft was an honourable and appropriate inheritance ensuring that whatever flights of architectural fancy the Adams might indulge in were firmly based on a foundation of good building practice.

William's father, John Adam, moved to Linktown of Abbotshall next to the burgh of Kirkcaldy, Fife, a thriving community which had been created a burgh of barony for a local landowner, Sir Andrew Ramsay, in 1663. Although there are only a few references to John's activities, mainly in the surviving records of the Hammermen of Linktown to whose recently-established Incorporation he paid his dues and in the building accounts of nearby Raith House, it is likely that he carried on a fairly substantial business as a mason-builder. The late seventeenth and early eighteenth centuries, with rebuilding and industrial development taking place in many localities, provided opportunities for speculative building, contracting and investment in allied industrial operations. It was in this age of new possibilities that William Adam grew up and set about finding his own feet in the trade.

He was baptised on 24 October 1689, the fifth and only surviving child of a family of eight born to John Adam and his wife, Helen Cranston whom he had married in Edinburgh in 1679. Helen was the second daughter of the late William, 3rd Lord Cranston, whose unfortunate political career during the Civil War and Commonwealth and his subsequent forfeiture had left his family in reduced circumstances, and the grand-daughter of the Earl of Leven for whom John Adam worked at Raith House in the 1690s. From his own account William was 'bred a mason and served his time as such' and as a young man he visited the Low Countries and parts of northern France. From Holland he brought home some practical ideas for widening the scope of his activities: a model of a barley mill and information about the manufacture of Dutch pantiles.

William Adam; by William Aikman, c.1727. *(Reproduced by permission of Keith Adam of Blair Adam. Photograph, Antonia Reeve)*

It is characteristic of him that even in his earliest days as a master craftsman he was involved in many aspects of his trade: mason work, measuring, surveying, the manufacture and supply of necessary raw materials such as bricks, tiles and timber, and investment in industries such as coal and salt works in Fife and the Lothians which increased his capital. His belief in having a stake in as many aspects of the building trade as possible was one which he passed on to his sons who grew up in the comfort provided by his success. His partner in the brick and tile manufactory at Linktown was William Robertson, formerly factor on the Wemyss estate, who had purchased the lands of Gladney near Cupar but settled in Linktown where he built himself a large residence which became known as Gladney House. In 1716 at the age of 27 William Adam married his partner's daughter, Mary, then aged 17, who became a capable and fitting partner for her energetic husband and a presiding matriarchal presence in the household during her widowhood.

In the summer of 1728, just after the birth of his second son, Robert, William had a visit from his patron, Sir John Clerk of Penicuik, who noted in his journal:

Entrance front, House of Dun, Angus. *(The National Trust for Scotland)*

'I took a little time to consider a brickwork belonging to Mr Adams, Architect. This I found as expensive a piece of work as the nature of it required and I could not enough admire the enterprising temper
of the proprietor who had at that time under his own care near to twenty general projects – Barley Mills, Coal Works, Salt Pans, Marble Works, Highways, Farms, houses of his own a-building and houses of others not a few'.

It is unlikely that William Adam became immersed in all these enterprises simply in order to become rich. The law agent of his client at Cally House in Galloway remarked,

'I... can assure you that his character here [Edinburgh] is that he is far from being a money catcher; on the contrary he is often bitt by the bargains he makes. He is certainly a great genius in his way and hath given proofs of it in our Royal Infirmary which is now almost finished and one of the grandest buildings of the age in our parts...'.[2]

The proceeds of his industrial undertakings and the raw materials they pro-

The hall, Arniston House, Midlothian; designed by William Adam, plasterwork executed by Joseph Enzer. *(Royal Commission on the Ancient and Historical Monuments of Scotland)*

duced provided much-needed support for his architectural practice; he claimed that he made only £300 profit from his work at Hopetoun over ten years. Besides, even a prosperous eighteenth-century businessman could have sudden problems of cash-flow and credit. In 1725 William wrote to Sir John Clerk for help

> *'with some Money Matters... for I trusted to a bill of my Lord Marchmont's for my timber I sold at Leith, and tho' I was assur'd of it at this term, Yet am put of for some time which in truth puts me to the greatest uneasiness... But Yor Lordship helping me Just now with a Hundred Pound ster. wou'd Make me Easy... I hope to Live and make a gratefull return'.*[3]

His role as 'undertaker' or builder as well as architect at his commissions gave him control over the realisation of his designs and the quality of the workmanship. Entrepreneurial flair and an eye to the main chance were important even when the ultimate aim was artistic rather than material advantage. It is easier to believe that William Adam's priority was professional rather than material in that it re-appeared so clearly in Robert who was, temperamentally and creatively, most of all the Brothers his father's son. In spite of his ambition and having headed a firm who today might almost have been millionaires, he remarked characteristically, 'the Divill take me if I ever leave myself a groat in this side of time', and he told the Edinburgh College Trustees that 'though the money is no indifferent object to me yet ... I have been infinitely more actuated by the motive of leaving behind me a monument of my talents, such as they are, than by any hope of gain whatever ...'.[4]

The public appointments that came William Adam's way were also a steady source of income, notably those of Clerk and Storekeeper of the Works in Scotland (1728) and Mason to the Board of Ordnance (1730), although his friends failed to secure for him the office of Surveyor of the King's Works in Scotland formerly held by James Smith. His practical advice was sought from time to time by public authority; in 1733 the Barons of Exchequer, who included his patron Sir John Clerk, called upon him to make a report on the condition of

Sir John Clerk of Penicuik, doyen of the gentlemen-amateur architects; after William Aikman. *(Trustees of the National Galleries of Scotland)*

Mavisbank House, Midlothian. *(Royal Commission on the Ancient and Historical Monuments of Scotland)*

the roof of Holyrood palace, describing him to the Treasury as 'a person of approved Skill and Integrity in Architecture'. The architect found that 'the Roof thereof is in a very ruinous and decayed Condition, and That from some Views had by Pulling down parts of the Ceiling, There is reason to believe the greatest Part of the Timbers of the said Fabrick are entirely decayed and destroyed';[5] the disaster was blamed on the parsimoniousness of an earlier repair. William gained lucrative contracts for building from the Ordnance Board, notably in connection with the building of fortifications in the Highlands after the Jacobite Risings. The work which he contracted for at Fort George passed on his death to John and his brothers for whom the annual 'campaign' to the Fort at Ardersier became a regular feature of their professional and social life.

William Adam's architectural practice developed dramatically in the 1720s as that of James Smith declined, flourishing in the patronage of an influential group of noblemen and landowners who included the Duke of Hamilton, the Earls of Stair and Hopetoun, the Marquess of Tweeddale, Lord Braco (later the Earl of Fife), David Erskine Lord Dun and Sir John Clerk of Penicuik. His work took him as far away as Galloway and Banffshire, Roxburghshire and Perthshire. He was sometimes commissioned to design and build an entirely new house, as at Mellerstain (Berwickshire), Mavisbank and Arniston (Midlothian) and Duff House (Banffshire), or asked to remodel an existing one, as at Yester (East Lothian) and Hopetoun (West Lothian). He was consulted as a landscape gardener at several houses, including Taymouth castle (Perthshire) and Buchanan House (Stirlingshire); an appreciation of the landscape setting of a house was also something that he passed on to his sons.

The bones of his houses, so to speak, may be Palladian but the flesh and blood of the grandest of them are vitalised by his enthusiasm for the architects of the Renaissance, some of whose books he collected for his library, and the Baroque which he had seen at first hand in Holland and France. Sometimes his work shows the influence of James Gibbs and of Sir John Vanbrugh whose work Robert and James Adam also admired. The exteriors of William Adam's houses are often

Drawing by an unidentified artist of the Bridge over the Tay at Aberfeldy, one of many public works carried out for the Ordnance Board by William Adam. 1797. *(The Trustees of the National Galleries of Scotland)*

more richly modelled and decorated than was advocated by the ultra-Palladians; the tall pilasters blossoming into rich Corinthian capitals at Duff House, the light and shade among the carving over the windows and door and on the pediment of Mavisbank, the classical urns punctuating the skyline at Hopetoun.

> '*I am of opinion*', he wrote to Sir John Clerk about his villa at Mavisbank, '*that one window in the Midle of the Pediement will have the best Effect with a Large piece of foliage on each Syde, & that all the Leaffs, flowers and fruits be very Large in being farr from the Eye... the more the foliage rises and the darker the shades are, So much the better att that distance*'.

Dramatic effect could be even more marked indoors where he could indulge his love of surface decoration to the full, as in the hall at Dun or Arniston.

He designed 8 major public buildings (besides lesser ones): town houses for Aberdeen, Dundee and Haddington, dignified classical versions of the old Scots tolbooth, Robert Gordon's Hospital in Aberdeen, that of George Watson and the Orphan Hospital in Edinburgh, the Edinburgh Royal Infirmary and the University library at Glasgow, more restrained than his private houses but fitting monuments to their purposes of civic charity and learning.

It was with a view to publicising his achievements even before 1730 that William planned the publication of a volume of his designs to be called *Vitruvius Scoticus*. Impetus was given to the project by his tour of English buildings in 1727, subscriptions began to be collected in the autumn of that year but by the following spring preparations slowed down and publication was suspended. John attempted to revive the project after his father's death but it was not until 1810 that an altered and enlarged version appeared. A modern edition, carefully edited and annotated in order to do justice to William Adam's own work, was published in 1980.

Having moved to Edinburgh soon after Robert's birth in 1728, when he was made a burgess *gratis* 'for good services', William acquired property in the over-

Mary Robertson, Mrs William Adam; by Allan Ramsay, c.1750s. *(Reproduced by permission of Keith Adam of Blair Adam. Photograph, Antonia Reeve)*

Robert Adam's early design for alterations to Blair House. Undated. *(Reproduced by permission of Keith Adam of Blair Adam. Photograph, the Royal Commission on the Ancient and Historical Monuments of Scotland)*

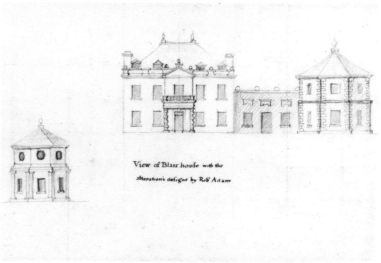

View of Blair house with the alterations designd by Robt Adam

crowded town including some lying off the Cowgate at the foot of Marlin's Wynd. Here he and his wife set up house and reared their large family of four sons and six daughters. In 1731 he bought the estate of Blair Crambeth in Kinross-shire, later renamed Blair Adam but known to the family as 'the Blair'. To this he added several adjoining properties between 1735 and 1747. It would be simplistic to see the purchase of an estate as mere social climbing. It was an old-established practice of merchants and professional men such as lawyers to buy land and architects had long been following their example. Land was more secure than moveable property however substantial. The coal beneath the lands of Blair Crambeth was one of its most attractive assets to William Adam who named the colliers' village Maryburgh after his wife and took it as his own territorial designation. The interest taken by him and his sons in the improvement of the policies surrounding the simple house which he built at first demonstrates their affection for it as a private retreat from the world of business, the ideal of so many eighteenth-century men of affairs. The gift to Robert of the ruined castle of Dowhill on the estate may have fanned his 'romantic imagaination' although his surviving youthful drawing for the enlargement of Blair House is classical.

The possession of a landed estate and the preoccupations of a country gentleman helped to make a professional architect socially acceptable to, if not the equal of, patrons of higher social origins. Their shared enthusiasm for antiquity and the modern architecture inspired by it created common intellectual and artistic ground in which friendship could grow. John Clerk of Eldin described William Adam as a man of 'distinguished genius, inventive enterprise and persevering application attended with a graceful, independent and engaging address which was remarked to command reverence from his inferiors, respect from his equals and uncommon friendship and attachment from men of the highest rank, among whom the great Earl of Stair was one, who seemed by a sympathy of character to be peculiarly destined for the friend and patron of such a man'.

In this cordial atmosphere William Adam could ask Sir John Clerk for a loan

Wash drawing of rocks and trees, signed 'M.A.' [Margaret Adam]. Undated. *(Reproduced by permission of Keith Adam of Blair Adam. Photograph, Royal Commission on the Ancient and Historical Monuments of Scotland)*

of books on architecture to fill gaps in his own considerable library and in the same letter recommend two 'necessitous persons' to Sir John's charity. Or he could ask the Duke of Hamilton, to whom he was both architect and industrial adviser, to do him the honour of witnessing the baptism of his son James. Yet, patrons had to be handled with tact, especially those gentlemen-amateurs who had arrived at a knowledge of the art by intellectual not practical routes, who were apt to look upon the professional architect as a consultant whose advice they were free to take or leave. Sir John Clerk, while planning his house of Mavisbank 'with Mr Adams a skilful architect' remarked in his journal, 'however the architecture may please or displease it is chiefly oweing to myself'. At times William Adam was prepared to follow the ideas of a knowledgeable patron at others he felt the need to insist on his own professional knowledge of what was best, even to change the plans as he saw fit. In 1725, in connection with progress at Redbraes, he wrote to Lord Marchmont:

> *'I have presum'd from the freedom Yor Lordship seem'd to alow me to make another plan, keeping als Closs by what Yor Lordship seem's to intend as possibly I cou'd – I have indeed ventur'd to advance the front wall 12 foot further Northward,... I promise my self that this 12 foot further Northward will be the more easily granted especially when itt Compleits the State of the first floor, And afoords two Ante Chambers or waiting rooms for Servants in the most propper places'.*

On another occasion he recommended to the Earl the use of stucco:

> *'it is a Plaister much us'd now in Publick rooms, such as the Hall, Dining Room, Parlour, etc., etc. And My Lord Burlington has done the floors of some of his rooms with itt in imitation of Marble. It can be made of any Colour, or vein'd as Marble – itt does Not suffer by washing, but rather hardens.... It is originally ane Alabase brunt as a Lymstone, and some pairt of itt Boyld, and immediately after Mixing with watter hardn's as a Stone.'*[6]

His energy, originality and experience must often have inspired confidence in his clients. In 1724, Lord Marchmont finding his house of Redbraes unfit to live in, arranged to get advice from various quarters including

> *'Lord Hopetoun's architect [William Adam] who no doubt is the best in Scotland, and have his advice about making it a good House, and let him be pay'd for his advice, then see if what I propose is practicable, and about what expence. Tho I should be glad to have a scheme from him and his advice first'.*[7]

There were times, however, when the volume of his business, which made it difficult to get hold of him, tried a client's patience. Writing to the Duke of Montrose's factor about the delay in improvements at Auchincloich, Walter Buchanan announced that 'Mr Adam is so throng else where that I cannot previl with him to return. So if you think fit to Desire him or upon his refusal to allow me to call another'.[8] The Marquess of Annandale was more outspoken in his exasperation:' as for Adams, he has so many real and so many imaginary projects that he minds nobody and nothing to purpose'.[9] The architect's relations with the Earl of Aberdeen for whom he worked at Haddo House were complicated by regular advice from Sir John Clerk who often acted as mentor to fellow-patrons. In 1733 John Baxter, the mason in charge at Haddo, saw fit to write to Sir John after a period of friction with William Adam:

> ' [the Earl] seis planly now that the storys Mr Adams advanced to him is false... for the house stands weill, without Crack or fla or the least simptem of a sitte in any part of the whoall So Mr Adams is disapointed who thought to have turned me of with disgrace and got the work all in his own hand'.[10]

Apparently some people felt that he was in danger of overstepping himself, equipped as he was to engross so many aspects of the building trade.

His most serious breakdown in relations with a client was with Lord Braco over the building costs of Duff House; 'a monstrous House' as the owner called it, having found that the original design 'comprehended a greater House than he had occasion for'. The house was founded in 1735 with work proceeding rapidly until 1741 when Lord Braco refused to pay the huge bill of £2500 sterling for the carving of capitals and other features which the architect on his own initiative had had carved in his own premises at Queensferry and shipped to Banff. The real cause of the dispute lay in the lack of a proper contract and firm arrangements about costs and labour between architect and client. The long legal battle that ensued during which William Adam defended himself vigorously in court, cast a shadow over his later career and was only settled in 1748 a few months before his death.[11] Lord Braco, whose known ostentatiousness may have encouraged his architect to plan on such a grand scale, declined to live in his incomplete house after what he called 'the barefaced villainy of Adams'. With characteristic loyalty, however, the Adam family remained particularly proud of Duff House, business failure or not. John Clerk of Eldin included it in a select list of his father-in-law's finest works, 'Braco's house' was among 'the best plans in Scotland' that Robert longed to have by him in Italy in 1756, in spite of his changing ideas, and on another occasion wrote of how in Rome Abbé Peter Grant had spoken of his father and 'Braco's' during their conversation. Artistic achievement, however loss-making in the short term, was what mattered in the end, although John Adam would have been more reluctant that Robert to subscribe to such a maxim.

GOD'S BEGETTING

The story was told in the Adam family of how one day as the children played in the garden of their home in the Cowgate, Robert as usual directing their games, a wall under which they had been sitting to eat their 'collation' collapsed seconds after they had jumped up at Robert's suggestion and run across the garden to sit in another spot. Apart from the irony that the Builder's bairns narrowly escaped being buried under the rubble of a badly-maintained wall in his own back yard, the tale is eloquent of Robert's role in the family.[12]

Being seven years younger than his older brother John he must have been the only big brother whom the younger Adams could remember as part of their childhood activities. John began helping his father in the office while Robert was still a schoolboy at the High School of Edinburgh. In 1750, two years after their father's death, when John married and set up his own establishment at Merchiston, Robert became resident head of the household in the Cowgate in the day to day sense until he left for his European tour in 1754, although both households were in close touch with each other. Robert was looked up to by two younger brothers, James and William (who were four and ten years his junior respectively), and a flock of sisters, Janet (Jenny), Elizabeth (Betty), Helen (Nelly), Mary, Susannah and Margaret (Peggy). His friends became their acquaintances, his enthusiasms their talking points and his talents a source of family pride. In a sense their personal attitudes to Robert and his activities were to determine the place of members of the family in the Adam story of success and failure. In the earliest days of the partnership of John and Robert the former held the family business on the profitable course set by their father, even increasing those profits. Robert, having found his personal footing during his study tour abroad gradually made the running and was eventually to transform the Adam practice into his own image just as his father had done a generation before.

John Clerk of Eldin's adulatory draft-biography of Robert, his brother-in-law and lifelong friend, gives details of his early life not recorded elsewhere. A physically frail child subject to debilitating bouts of a fever which followed him into his twenties, Robert appears to have been a bright schoolboy and university student who naturally shared his interests with the captive audience of his closely-knit family. His earliest pastime is said to have been, not surprisingly, building things, including the seat under the ill-fated garden wall, followed by the perennial boyish interest in weapons of warfare, in his case constructing cannon and fortifications. In common with his brothers John and James and at least one sister, Peggy, drawing became a favourite activity. John Clerk tells us that Robert's greatest pleasure in his teens lay in architecture and painting but that of the two he would have liked most to be a painter. All three brothers have left not only early drawings of classical houses, as one would expect from their father's sons, but also of various Gothic buildings, probable and fanciful, which caught their imaginations. In a journal of a visit to London in 1749 with Robert, James, Jenny and his Mother, John noted: 'We arrived at Tweedmouth... there was a sketch on the wall of the bedroom where we lay, of a Gothic Spire, among the prettyest things of the kind I have seen'.[13]

Robert's university days ended after only about two years following a serious illness. This was in 1745, the year in which Prince Charles Edward's army briefly occupied the burgh. The College students, including the Adams' friend Alexander Carlyle, formed a body of Volunteers and helped Robert's favourite professor Colin Maclaurin to strengthen the defences of the burgh walls. During the Jacobite occupation William Adam 'thought it prudent' to retreat to the Blair, taking John with him, in company with his brother-in-law and business associate Archibald Robertson, known affectionately in the family circle as 'Uncle Bauldie'. This move may have been in order to distance themselves from the stance of Robertson's Jacobite relatives. One aspect of Robert's socialising in Rome which was to worry Mrs Adam at first was his hobnobbing with Jacobites, until he reassured her that crowds went to see the Cardinal of York at prayer, that he had not even glimpsed 'James how's he cau'd [the Old Pretender]' and that 'the best Whigs' visited Dr Irvine, the Pretender's doctor, who asked him to dine.

Pressure of business caused William Adam to take his two oldest sons in turn from their academic studies in order to help him. John at least, according to his father, had a good practical training, 'bred up in the knowledge of Carpenter work, as well as mason work and architecture'. He acted as his father's amanuensis in business correspondence. It was John whom William Adam sent to important meetings in London with the Duke of Argyll and the Ordnance Board but according to John Clerk of Eldin Robert was often included in his father's discussions with clients, including the Earl of Hopetoun 'with whom he was something of a favourite'. There are brief glimpses of a felicitous relationship between father and sons and his pleasure at their developing talents. John Clerk relates how during one of Robert's illnesses, after Mrs Adam had given the Doctor an account of his constitution his father added 'with the greatest warmth' that 'he had the sweetest disposition with the finest genius'. William Adam's last surviving letter to Roger Morris, about the Garron Bridge, Inveraray, contains a touch of fatherly pride:' John is not a little vain of the confidence reposed in him as to the fixing of the proportions and if doubts arise will communicate his thoughts to you'.

Drawing of a Gothic tower by Robert Adam, 1753. *(Reproduced by permission of Keith Adam of Blair Adam. Photograph, the Royal Commission on the Ancient and Historical Monuments of Scotland)*

The year 1748 must have seen Robert plunged into greater personal responsibilities. His father's failing health since the previous winter and John's absence in London early in 1748 must have added to these, while he was still under twenty. That summer John again travelled on business, some of it in the north of Scotland, and was actually away from home when his father died on 24 June. It fell to Robert to intimate the event to friends. His letter to Lord Milton, the Justice Clerk, was written the next day:

> *'As you was long pleased to honor my Father with your Countenance & regard and as I have often heard him mention your Name with the greatest respect and gratitude, I thought it my duty to inform your Lordship That Yesternight we were deprived of him for ever. My brother John's untimely Absence Obliges us to delay his Buriall for a few days But so soon as we have fixed the time We shall take the liberty to inform your Lordship of it'.*[14]

William Adam was buried in Greyfriars' churchyard where his sons designed a mausoleum for his tomb. His obituaries in lamenting his loss also looked to the future:

> *'His genius for architecture push'd him out of Obscurity into a high Degree of Reputation. and his Activity of Spirit, not to be confined within narrow Bounds, diffused itself into many Branches of Business, not more to his own benefit than to that of his native country. As to the latter, 'tis fortunate he has left behind him some promising young men to carry on what he has so happily begun. Their regard for so worthy a Man, their Parent, will be to them a more than ordinary Incitement to tread in his steps; for he was a good Artist, but a still better man'.*

Arniston House, Midlothian;
William Adam, c. 1726
(*Royal Commission on the
Ancient and Historical
Monuments of Scotland*)

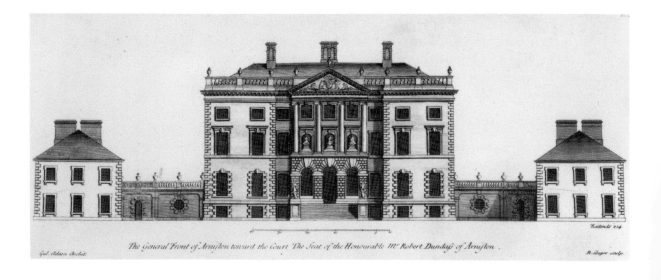

The General Front of Arniston toward the Court The Seat of the Honourable Mr Robert Dundas of Arniston.

For John there was added to the personal loss the burden of carrying on the family's many-sided practice, no small responsibility for a twenty-seven-year-old even though he immediately took his younger brother into partnership. The existence of well-established contacts in the building trade and the continuing presence in the office of their father's chief clerk 'Sanders' White must have been a comfort in the early days. Thanks to the influence of sympathetic friends, such as Robert Barclay of Collairnie who was moved by the family's 'Disconsolate condition' to write on their behalf to Lord Milton, the contracts with the Ordnance Board were renewed to John. There were private clients to be reassured of the firm's attention, especially those whose work had slowed down due to William Adam's recent inability to get around. Six days after his father's death John wrote to the 2nd Duke of Montrose, client at Buchanan House, one of many such letters which he must have dispatched about this time.

'My Lord, As your Grace was long pleased to honour my Father with your Countenance and Protection', he wrote, echoing the words of Robert's letter to Lord Milton, 'I recon it my Duty to take this first Opertunity since my return from the north Countrey, of informing your Grace of the irreparable Loss his Family sustain'd by his Death, which happend on Friday last. I would fain presume to hope, from your Grace's former Goodness to him, You will be pleased still to bestow some part of it on his Children'.[15]

Some sense of the crisis caused by William Adam's death may be gained from the Duke's letters to his agent in the following summer and autumn.

'On Monday last', he wrote on 7 July 1748, 'I dined in town [London] and then heard that Mr Adams was dead, which is confirmed to me by a letter I just now got from his Son, ... I am sorry for the man, also for his family to whom he will be an irreparable loss, he was very ingenious and undoubtedly the most sufficient in his profession of any in Scotland, so that the want of him must disconcert many people for some time'.

He suggested asking Lord Hopetoun's advice on John's abilities:

'...their [sic] *might be no hurt in letting Ld Hopetoun (as he has been very obliging in the affair) know my inclinations & disposition to incourage the Young Man, if he who is a judge thinks him a proper person & of sufficient skill & experience...'.*[16]

Lord Hopetoun was most reassuring.

'Poor William Adam's death is truly a general loss,' he wrote to the Duke, *'and the more so that there is nobody in this Country in the smallest degree equall to him. His son John is I am sure much preferable to any other being a Lad of very good parts and sense, unwearied Application and perfectly Sober; of Knowledge in Business far beyond his Years. I cannot say I ever thought him quite so quick as his Father, indeed very few are, but I'm persuaded his Modesty helped to make him appear less so, than he really is; and upon the whole I can venture to assure your Grace that he is abundantly qualified to execute all you have in View & to undertake that he will serve you honestly... he has likewise a Brother, a very clever Lad and well advanced that will be a great Assistance to him'.*[17]

It is a tribute to William Adam's training of his sons that the Earl was able to give them this testimonial. John, of course, had several years in the office behind him when the Earl had succeeded his own father in 1742. Lord Hopetoun had evidently had time to observe Robert's abilities after less than three years' training. By the winter of 1748-9, however, the Duke of Montrose was fretting at John's non-appearance at Buchanan;

'if he turns out as unsettled as his father, I must look for some other person to employ for I will not dance attendance on a person who I am willing to pay well for wateing on me, and who will get a very good thing if my works go on'.

In early February John wrote a detailed letter to the factor, Graham of Gorthy about preparations for the spring building season including the cutting in advance of hewn work for the doors, windows and chimneys, 'which ought to be in some forwardness before the building begins, as few hands laying soon consume a great quantity of hewn work'. Although the work at Buchanan went slowly on the Duke was complaining in March that he was convinced 'Adams looks upon my works as the least worth notice of those he is concerned with'.

The major private commission carried over from William Adam's lifetime was Hopetoun House. It is now thought, from the dating and general style of the work carried on under John's direction, including those changes to the exterior decided upon but still not executed when his father died and the decoration of the great state rooms, that Robert may have had little to do with it.18 In the absence of the necessary evidence it is impossible to be certain how much responsibility for work in progress was delegated to him by John who, as head of the firm, conducted their business correspondence with the Earl and took the major decisions. If John Clerk of Eldin is to be believed Robert had often been drawn into discussions with the Earl even during William Adam's lifetime yet the Earl's opinion of him, as conveyed to the Duke of Montrose, is unlikely to have been formed solely in conversation. To say that he was 'well advanced' in the practice of his profession suggests that Lord Hopetoun had seen for himself what Robert could do, even by 1748. His involvement if any may have been connected with the completion of the exterior which appears to have been finished in 1751. Both brothers were on the move in the summer of 1752. They were together at Fort George early that summer and later John stayed on there alone giving Robert the chance to take a short holiday at Moffat spa with the rest of the family. Soon tiring, however, of the 'dances, bowls and scandal' there, as he once described it, and possibly feeling the pull of his sketch books and the open country he set off over the Border into Cumberland.

'Where think You this wandering rogue Bob is got to', wrote John with understandable impatience from Fort George on 1 July to Peggy, who was still on holiday, *'a Visit to the Moffat won't serve his turn, but he must jaunt away to Carlisle also. I hope my letter... arrived safe at Edinburgh and was forwarded to him by express to Moffat and would be there time enough to catch him before he went off on his rambles. I am very sorry that things turned out so as I could have been obliged to beg him to come so soon North again. But necessity has no law, and I do not well know which way to get everything made out'.*[19]

In the summer of 1753 Robert himself did duty at Fort George, while in the summer and autumn of 1754 he was at Dumfries House and Inveraray. There would, therefore, seem little time left for his attendance at Hopetoun where, now that the exterior was finished, work on the hall, private and great dining rooms and great drawing room had begun.

Paul Sandby, 'South Prospect of Leith'; pen and black ink and watercolour, Edinburgh 1749. *(The Ashmolean Museum, Oxford)*

It may even be the case, although this is little more than speculation, that he was out of sympathy with the work that was going ahead, much of which appears to have been derived from the pattern books of Isaac Ware. When in 1755 the Earl of Hopetoun sent to Italy for a design for a chimney-piece for what became the red drawing room, Robert dashed one off in a hurry, 'only… as an idea of the thing without any pretensions to extraordinary', also based on a Ware design. It would have been characteristic of him to regard it as hardly worthwhile to contribute an original design to a scheme which he had had little to do with and may not have cared for. When the Earl's pleasure in his sketch was reported to him by John, he remarked in a letter home, 'which shows how much a trifle from Italy will impose, even on a sensible man'. However, he did not intend to cut himself off from Hopetoun completely;

'I intend to give his Lordship another letter soon to keep up the familiarity betwixt us, and Crack some Italian jokes with him, and propose to him to pull down his whole House that I may have the satisfaction to try my genius on a new one'.

It was also partly with tongue in cheek but with an element of seriousness too that he reported a conversation between himself and Charles Hope after a day on which they had surprised each other by the companionable mood in which they had 'roll'd about together from morning to night' looking at the churches and palaces of Rome. Hope, he declared,

'has got the same notion of my improvements with many here and has no doubts of my making the first Architect in Britain. He told me my Lord [Hopetoun] would not be for my returning to Scotland as he would be afraid of my finding fault with everything about Hopetoun House and with my dictatorial Authority, making him do a thousand things that he would wish to avoid. I told him that was very possible and that I had already thought of a Scheme for his Library, which would make it one of the finest things in the World, I explain'd my Scheme to him and he agreed it woud, but said I must Make his Brother think it was his own contrivance'.[20]

Dumfries House, Ayrshire, main front; founded in the summer of 1754 before Robert Adam left for Italy. *(Royal Commission on the Ancient and Historical Monuments of Scotland)*

In the event the Earl did better for Robert than allowing him to make his mark on Hopetoun by suggesting the visit to Italy where he worked out his own destiny.

He had much more personal responsibility, at least in the early stages, for the partnership's commission to build a new house in Ayrshire for the Earl of Dumfries, for whom the Earl of Hopetoun acted as mentor in choosing them as architects and judging the suitability of their designs. The new house which had first been suggested in 1747 but was delayed partly by William Adam's death the following year, partly by the Earl's hesitation over the plans and haggling over the estimate was not founded until the summer of 1754. Only one drawing, for a minor building in the grounds in the form of a temple, is signed by Robert, and there is now no way of telling whether those other drawings which were finally accepted were also by him. The cutback in expenditure and simplification of the plans may account for the externally plain house which was built. The inspiration of the fine rococo designs for the plasterwork ceilings, characteristic of the firm's work at this time, has been traced to either Ware again or the work of the rococo artist William de la Cour who had painted arabesques and landscapes for John Adam at Lord Milton's house in Edinburgh in 1748. A week after the laying of the foundation stone on 18 June an advance payment of £1,500 was made to Robert who stayed on to superintend the first stage of the work, at the same time enjoying every minute of the Earl's house-party that was gathered to celebrate the founding. 'I thought to have wrote you by Tuesday's post', he apologised to his mother on 11 August, 'but really was so occupied in drinking and seeing nothing that it was not in my power to fulfil my intentions .... we are always merry and laughing'. His personal connection with Dumfries House ended when he left for Italy but as late as 1758, after he was settled in London, he was anxious to learn how much he was due from the profits;

'*Willie says Sanders Whyte [John's chief clerk] told him that I cou'd not know what I was to draw from that till the whole was finished nor cou'd he make up my Accounts on that Score, pray send me a Copy of My account ...*', he wrote to James in Edinburgh.[21]

In the north of Scotland in the late 1740s and early 1750s the firm's work centred around their building contract with the Ordnance Board which was the most lucrative part of their business. This was especially so after work began on the massive Fort George, relocated from Inverness where it had been planned to build it in their father's time to the Ardersier peninsula on the Moray Firth. The building of the fort, in masonry and brickwork, on a strategically excellent but technically difficult site, is a credit to the high standards of workmanship imposed by John and Robert, and a little later James, during their spells of personal supervision. The operation also involved the shipment of building materials to a specially constructed pier – one of the ships, named 'The Adams of Fort George', doubled as a piece of business promotion for the firm. Brick kilns and various workshops were set up and a labour-force of as many as 1000 workmen and soldiers was at times necessary during major tasks of earth removing. Supervising these operations was no sinecure for the Adams involving them in long journeys to and from Ardersier where they lived in a 'brick habitation' with mostly the military for company. Now and again a friend would find his way there or welcome visits might be made to local families. Robert and James made acquaintances among the officers and their womenfolk and were somewhat scathing about the (according to them) unsophisticated young ladies whom the engineer-in-charge and his wife, Colonel and Mrs Skinner, invited along to decorate the dinner parties. Colonel William Skinner, designer of the fort, tended on his bad days to treat the superior young Adams like glorified bricklayers, or so they felt, while the wife of one of the Officers left Robert unaccustomedly speechless one

John Adam; by Francis Cotes, c.1750. *(Reproduced by permission of Keith Adam of Blair Adam. Photograph, Antonia Reeve)*

day by telling him to his face that she could never stand any of his family except 'the old woman Adams'.

It is from Fort George that the Brothers' earliest long letters home have survived. Unfortunately their letters concerned with the progress of work at the Fort, which were probably retained in the office at Edinburgh, have vanished and the handful that remain are personal letters to their sisters; 'we have remained very busy', Robert told Peggy on one occasion, 'doing what my letter to John will Inform you of, if you want to know or think you will understand'. He did report on his daily attempts to avoid the 'flashes, furies and madnesses of that most ridiculous of mortals', Colonel Skinner. He wrote to his sister Jenny in May 1753 on his arrival at the Fort:

James Adam; by Allan Ramsay, c.1750. *(The Laing Art Gallery, Newcastle-upon-Tyne)*

Fort George, Ardersier, on the Moray Firth; an annual training ground in the art of good building for Robert Adam and his brothers in the 1750s. *(Scottish Development Department)*

Buchanan House, Stirlingshire; general plan of a House and Offices, undated. William Adam was paid £315 for a plan and estimate in 1741 but his failing health meant that little was done. John Adam, whom the Duke commissioned to proceed with the new Offices in 1748, did substantial work in the 1750s; Robert's designs for further improvements, for which he was paid in 1770, were not executed. After later alterations the house was burnt in 1850. Another, built on a new site, was also burnt, in 1954. *(Vitruvius Scoticus, Plate 135: Royal Commission on the Ancient and Historical Monuments of Scotland)*

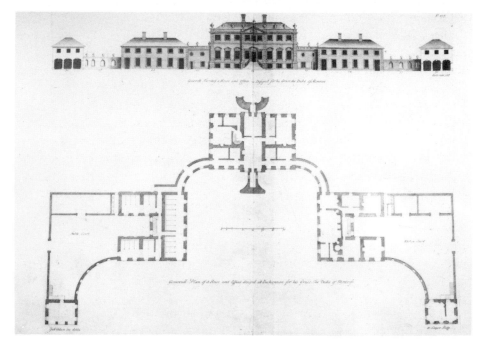

'I must Observe that on the Road I paid only for my Horses, as Mr Skinner would not take anything from me for Eating, So that you find I am a Sort of favorite at Present ... Mrs Skinner likes this place extreamly well and dislikes all the Beautys of Inverness as much as I do ... she criticizes every thing and every Body and like the Masculine Englishes esteems her Belly her cheif Good ... I believe I shall neither entertain Man, Woman and Child with any of my two polite qualifications of singing and Dancing till I see you, for ought I can see at present'.

The summer months in the North appear to have provided Robert with the opportunity to indulge in his favourite pastime of landscape painting, to judge by his memoranda of 1750 on the sketchbook which he carried on his tour of England that year; a List of 'Things to Carry to Ardersier' included 'My Book of Sketches' and 'Colours in an Ivory Case'. It was while at Fort George in 1753 that he is said to have received his first commission, a house in Nairn for Dr Mackenzie, factor to Rose of Kilravock. The doctor's son Henry (author of *The Man of Feeling*) later noted it as the work of 'Mr Adams then a very young artist', being 'the first house he ever planned'.[22]

Through contacts made during their Ordnance work some private commissions were undertaken in the North of Scotland in the 1750s by 'John Adam and Company'. This included the rebuilding of Banff Castle for Lord Deskford between 1750 and 1752 and alterations at Castle Grant in Morayshire for Sir Ludovic Grant of Grant begun in 1753, where John made further additions ten years later. The work at Banff Castle for Lord Deskford with whom Robert and James were particularly friendly, is recorded in letters and detailed accounts for materials, workmanship, craftsmen's travelling expenses and the carriage and sea-freight of everything from timber and bricks to marble and paint, the stone chimney-pieces and other carved work also having been prepared in Edinburgh. Construction work included a covered passage linking the old house with the new, the latter harled to protect it against the north-east weather. The total bill, discharged in the names of John and Robert, amounted to just under £1,696. The alterations at Castle Grant begun in 1753 with the recommendation of Lord Hopetoun, by which time the architects' partnership consisted of John, Robert and James, included the great 80-feet long north addition, part of constructions which eventually enveloped the old Castle. The rejuvenated stronghold of the Laird of Grant, magnificent of its kind, was a far cry from the Baroque splendour of Hopetoun. These northern commissions were part of the long association of William Adam and his sons with the Earls of Findlater and Seafield and their relatives; the 5th Earl of Findlater, 2nd Earl of Seafield was the brother-in-law of their patron Lord Hopetoun. Another commission spanning the two generations was Arniston, Midlothian, where John worked on the public rooms on the west side of the house between about 1753 and 1755. Robert was in contact with the client, Robert Dundas, just before leaving for Italy in the autumn of 1754 when he may have designed a Gothic bridge.[23]

Much of the business that passed through the Adam office, both while Robert

Letter from John Adam to Sir Ludovic Grant about work at Castle Grant, 29 March 1753. He asks on behalf of the 'very sober' overseer, David Frew, that the latter may be lodged at the Castle rather than at a public house. *(SRO, Seafield Muniments: GD248/176/1/25. Reproduced by permission of Seafield Estates)*

was still at home and after he left for Italy in 1754 but was still due his share as John's partner, included good bread-and-butter work: a report on why the bridge at Cullen might be in a state of near-collapse, a survey of an Edinburgh house formerly belonging to the executed Jacobite, Lord Lovat, which the Commissioners for the Annexed Estates wished to use as an office, or a site-investigation and plan for the Managers of a proposed new Concert Room the commission for which eventually went to their rival Robert Mylne. John Adam unfailingly treated clients' problems, however mundane, with courtesy and wrote careful, lucid explanations in reply. The Countess of Findlater's S.O.S. about the bridge at Cullen, forwarded by her brother Lord Hopetoun, contained a sketch drawn by a local tradesman to show the bridge's present state. John returned several pages of 'Observes upon the Plan & Description of the failure in the litle Bridge att Cullen; With a method proposed for helping the same', and a drawing depicting the rescued bridge with handsome new buttresses. 'The new Drawings that I have made out are by a larger scale, that they may be the more intelligible'.[24] John's conscientiousness occasionally prompted him to give his client preventative as well as remedial advice; in writing his report of a visit to Balnagowan House he felt obliged to point out to Captain John Ross how badly the trees in his coppices needed pruning and suggested he order his gardener to do something about it.[25]

The firm's major work as builders, not designers, apart from Fort George, in which the Brothers took a share before Robert went abroad was that at Inveraray

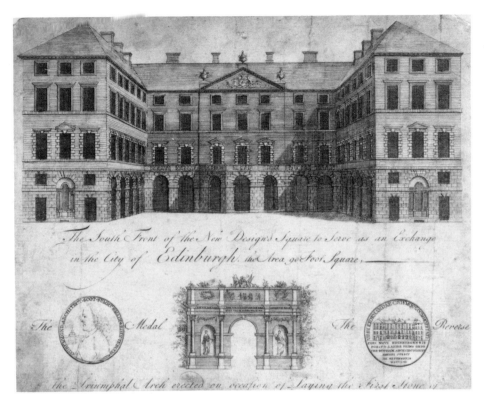

Design for the South Front of the new Exchange, Edinburgh; John Adam, 1753. The construction of the building was handed over to a group of builders. *(Royal Commission on the Ancient and Historical Monuments of Scotland)*

Castle for the political manager the Duke of Argyll. On 13 July 1746, about two years after the laying of the foundation stone, the Duke's agent, Campbell of Stonefield, wrote to him expressing his joy that work was to go forward on the family house after a delay partly caused by the Jacobite Rising. Seemingly unaware that, thanks to the influence of Lord Milton with Argyll, William Adam had already been put in touch with the architect Roger Morris with a view to his taking on the supervision of the work, Stonefield recommended:

> 'If you have not already some other person in View, you know that Mr Adams the Architect is Considered as the ablest man we have in Scotland for Carrying on so great a Design ... There is one John Douglas at Edinburgh next in Character to Mr Adams, he has built several houses but never so great designs as this ...'.[26]

Superintendence at Inveraray was renewed to John on his father's death. In 1748, in commending him to Montrose, Lord Hopetoun remarked:

> 'I think it no bad proof of his Capacity that Morris with whom he was some Months at Inverara last year, has wrote to him that he has satisfied the Duke of Argyle of it, and that he is to have the carrying on of that work ...'.

Robert was with John at the Castle in the autumn of 1754. When John left to go on to Dumbarton to meet Colonel Skinner about Ordnance business Robert reported to their Mother that the Duke had at last settled affairs with them, giving them £300 for their trouble 'from the very beginning'. Not having expected it they were grateful. 'The Duke say'd that we had behaved vastly genteely and that he was obliged to us'. William Adam had failed to agree a fee with Argyll and John, who disliked haggling, had left the matter to the discretion of the Duke and Lord Milton. Until 1761 the construction of the great neo-Gothic Castle and the development of the town of Inveraray itself was to be a demanding commitment for John Adam as head of the firm. The Brothers' familiarity with Morris's design, so different from those produced in their father's office, may have been one source of their fascination with the Gothic at this time.

Archibald Campbell, 3rd Duke of Argyll (1682-1761), builder of Inveraray Castle and patron of the Adams; by Allan Ramsay. *(Trustees of the National Galleries of Scotland)*

John Adam, 'Design for a new approach to Edinburgh, 1752'. *(The British Architectural Library, R.I.B.A., London, L12/2)*

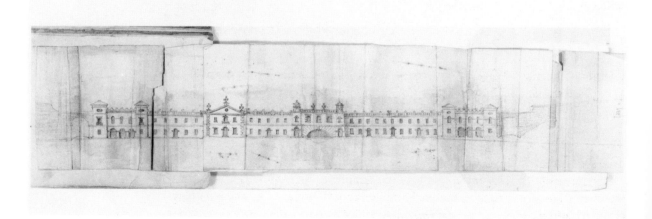

A WONDERFULLY
LOVING FAMILY

The Adams grew up between two worlds, the 'mechanick things' of the building trade and the polite society of their patrons. William Adam, having both practical experience of his craft and an appreciation of the philosophical sources of his art, was neither born gentleman nor mere operative. With a combination of business enterprise and creative ability he achieved his own professional and social standing. There were other self-made men in his field – the Mylnes were in the same position and had a longer record of service to the crown – but the scale of William Adam's operations marked him out as Scotland's 'universal architect'. His sons had the advantage of being born into the position that he had acquired for them, which included access to social circles otherwise above their station in 18th-century terms and a higher education, however brief, which brought them into contact with like-minded contemporaries from different social backgrounds, some of whom like themselves had to earn their living.

A constant stream of friends, many of whom Robert retained for life, was made welcome in the overflowing Adam household in the Cowgate (ten brothers and sisters with 21 years between the oldest and the youngest). After John married Jean Ramsay, daughter of a Kirkcaldy merchant, in 1750, and moved out to Merchiston there were two centres of family activity, John keeping his drawing office in the Cowgate family home. William, the youngest son, was sent off to school at Haddington, as John had earlier been sent to Dalkeith, and was afterwards apprenticed in the office of the banker, Adam Fairholm. Mary married the Rev John Drysdale and set up house in the manse at Kirkliston. Dr Alexander Carlyle (1722-1805), then a young minister at Inveresk, remembered the Adams as 'a wonderfully loving family' and John Clerk, Baron Clerk's seventh son who started life as an Edinburgh merchant and married Susannah Adam in 1753, described how 'the uninterrupted cordiality in which they lived, their conciliatory manners and the various accomplishments in which they severally made proficience, formed a most attractive society ...'.

Some of Robert's earliest friends were nearer his brother John in age, which seems to suggest the precociousness hinted at by John Clerk which gained him entry to the literary, philosophical and artistic conversations of his seniors, including his father's friends and clients. At the start of their careers in the early 1750s were his cousin William Robertson (1721-93) who lived much in the Adam household after the death of his parents and became minister of Gladsmuir in 1743; Alexander Carlyle who became minister at Inveresk in 1746 the year Robert probably left university; Adam Smith (1723-90) from Kirkcaldy, who lectured at Edinburgh University from 1748-51; Gilbert Elliot (1722-77), grandson of the judge, Lord Minto, who had been at school with John at Dalkeith and became MP for Selkirkshire in 1753; John Home (1722-1808) who became minister at Athelstaneford in 1746 but whose literary preoccupations caused him to rock the ecclesiastical establishment with his play *Douglas* while Robert was in Italy, driving him towards a secular career; and the Gaelic-speaking Adam Ferguson (1723-1816), also ordained to the ministry, who is said to have been a 'particular friend' of Robert, although five years his senior, who left home to become chaplain to the Black Watch Regiment while Robert was still at University. Already distinguished was the young philosopher and historian, David Hume (1711-76), the support of whose comfortable gentry family left him free to follow his own literary interests. 'That Family', he wrote of the Adams, 'is one of the few to whose Civilities I have been much beholden, and I retain a lively sense of them'. Hume was socially welcome for his genial personality and admired for his literary success. Discussion of his philosophical propositions among Robert's circle of friends, philosophers, poets and liberal-minded young clerics, must have been stimulating, although others found them disconcerting. The story is well known of how he charmed the redoubtable Mrs Adam at supper after Robert had infiltrated him without introduction, having been forbidden by his mother 'to bring the Atheist here to disturb my peace'. Thereafter she made 'the large jolly man who sat beside me' as welcome as the rest, having found him 'the most innocent, agreeable, facetious man I ever met with'. The family did not let her forget the incident; 'Compliments to your Mother honest woman and tell her that Davie Home is very much thought of by the Englishers', wrote John Clerk from London in 1756.

Artistic friends had more influence on Robert's personal accomplishments; his lifelong fellow-enthusiast and sketching companion, John Clerk (1728-1812), who became his brother-in-law; John 'Fatty' McGowan (d.1803), son of an Edinburgh lawyer, collector of antiquities, who became involved with the School of Design founded in Edinburgh in 1760, and the young Englishman Paul Sandby (1731-1809), both of whom were at home in the Adam household where they flirted with Robert's younger sisters and helped to encourage his own landscape painting and connoisseurship of art. Paul Sandby spent five years (1747-52) in Scotland as official draughtsman with William Roy who carried out the military survey of the Highlands for the Ordnance Board under General David Watson between 1747 and 1755. It was inevitable that he should become familiar with the family of the Ordnance builder William Adam, with whom he shared an enthusiasm for landscape painting and the experience of travelling through the Highlands where, as Sandby's son later put it, one 'saw nature in her wildest state'. As well as the many landscape drawings and figure studies which he made

See overleaf:

A proper repository, the ceiling of the Adam Dome, the General Register House, Edinburgh, executed c.1785; the central feature of Robert's first major public building in Scotland (Scottish Record Office; photograph by M Brookes).

The Trades Hall, Glassford Street, Glasgow; drawn by J Knox, engraved by J Swan. Robert Adam's plans for the development of central Glasgow were cut short by his death. The exterior of the Trades Hall, in spite of alterations, is a reminder of his plans for the city.

at this time Sandby also experimented with etching, which interested John Clerk. It was probably as a water-colourist that Sandby impressed Robert most and may have passed on to him the 'hints' on mixing colours which he jotted down in his notebook before a journey to Fort George.

Like many Scots families the Adams were both emotionally and financially dependent on one another well into adulthood. Whatever happened to one affected all, even the level-headed John confessing to being one of those 'born with Anxious tempers' when family letters became overdue. The household after William Adam's death was a benevolent matriarchy; the David Hume episode suggests that Mrs Adam's injunctions could be circumvented by appeals to her good nature. Robert when writing from Italy habitually parried her rebukes in a vein of affectionate effrontery, excusing himself on one occasion for not writing to her personally, 'as I know she looks on every thing address'd to her Children as address'd to herself'.

'My dear Mother', he admitted at New Year 1756 in reply to her censures of his riotous living in the Eternal City, *'it is certain I am rather Graceless but as I am in constant resolution to amend my ways and that I think there is plenty of time, I doubt not but I shall be enabled to keep the Commandments of God well at last, as you may remember I spent no short time in the study of them ... There are no Bibles to be got in this place, as I fancy that is forbid by the Church, and it is not my fault that I have not read a chapter morning and evening in imitation of Lord Hopetoun and the other exemplary lives of our native land ... I doubt not but you will have great reason to be pleased with me and to bless the Lord for giving you such a son amongst all his other mercies'.*

Mrs Adam's few letters, written from Moffat, where she and Jenny went together in 1753, or from Mary's home at Kirkliston, are brusque and to the point with more comments on what was happening at home than on what she was doing herself.

'Margrat my woman', she wrote to her youngest daughter from Moffat, *'As I have write a scrall to all the rest I shall write this to you, ... I fore gote to tel all you three young folks before I left the towne not to go with any young Gentlemen unless you had some married Lady to escort you, young folks carectour is verey soon hurt ...'.*

Her prohibition may have been prompted by an earlier escapade in which Susannah, Betty and Nelly went unaccompanied to a concert after which they received the following rhyme from an anonymous 'young Gentleman', possibly Paul Sandby who was given to versifying:

'The Sick P_____r sends his Comp's
To three ungracious giddy romps
He hopes that Susy, Bets and Nelly
For going o'er their Mother's Belly
To St Cecilia in such Weather
Have Penance all endur'd together.

He hopes that Sue was handed out
By Sixty limping with the Gout
That Betsy could not hear the Singer
Because a Fop did squeeze her finger,
That Nell (pray heav'n it mayn't dispatch her)
Receiv'd not one kind Glance from _____.

Yet hopes no headach, Prinkle, Cholick
Have follow'd on so rash a Frolick'

Society, 23 Novr. 1752.

Robert's comments on his sisters' progress in learning French have left brief pen-portraits of four of them; Jenny, he hoped, would have got over all the 'fyke facks' of it, Helen with her 'love of the polite world' would enjoy it, Betty 'with her unwearied application' would work hard, as would 'Miss Meggy with her natural parts and from the mirth and fun to be always carried on during the time of study'. Unlike their cousins, William Robertson's sisters, who like many Edinburgh girls from professional and mercantile families had to support themselves as shopkeepers and milliners, the Adam girls remained comfortably provided for at home, but with no independence. It was to be the fate of three of these lively girls, Jenny, Betty and Peggy, to become their brothers' housekeepers in London, sharing their triumphs and difficulties of over 30 years and treasuring the family correspondence which throws so much light on their architectural careers. Although they remained affectionately attached to their brothers, especially Robert of whose achievements they were immensely proud, they avoided fashionable society, finding their friends mainly among other Scots expatriates and lived retiring lives; 'God knows my time is not very precious', Betty once wrote wearily in the early days in London. She and her sisters deserve to be remembered for their supporting roles in the Adam story.

In the late 1740s and 1750s the Edinburgh office was firmly under the direction of John in the same way as Robert was later to lead his own team in London. Robert was John's second-in-command as James was to become his. 'Tell Bob that I ... pardon him for superior merit', James conceded as the London practice took off, 'I am much less ambitious than Caesar, I am contented to hold a second place'.[27] We have no way of knowing how Robert felt as junior partner in the Edinburgh office. There is little record of his personal contribution. It is a pity that his early plan for Dr Mackenzie's house at Nairn, with its annotations, is presently untraced. The partners' surviving correspondence with clients is written by John and accounts receipted with their joint names are probably in an office hand. Robert may have designed the interior decorations of Dumfries House, being closely concerned with the beginning of the work, but the plasterwork has been compared to that at Hopetoun of the 1750s which is most likely to have been executed under John's direction. The 'lightness' of the plasterwork in these houses, in contrast to the higher-relief, exuberant style of William Adam, may be a synthesis arrived at by the brothers but it is likely to have required John's final approval. The designs have been said to show a fairly direct use of contemporary pattern books, a characteristic of John, rather than early signs of the originality with which Robert was to use the classical sources which he studied at first hand in Italy. He certainly did his share of the work at Fort George and travelled with John to their scattered private commissions and work for the Ordnance Board.

Robert must have learned to respect the methods and standards of his more experienced brother during the eight years or so that they worked together. Their early drawings show a similar architectural style, partly learned in their father's office and partly inspired by those Palladian houses which they saw on their respective English visits: John in 1748, both of them during a family journey to London late in 1749 and Robert in 1750.[28] Both also remarked on Gothic buildings on their travels and made drawings in that style, which may have appealed more to their imagination than the classical manner which was associated with work. So marked was Robert's enthusiasm for it that his friend and tutor in Italy, the Frenchman Clérisseau, claimed that he was 'very ignorant of architecture when he came to me, except the Gothic: but I put him off that and gave him some taste for the antique'.[29] He and John also shared a love of landscape but whereas John's interest sought a mainly practical outlet in estate improvement (his letters reveal a genuine love of growing things), Robert increasingly saw the landscape as complementing buildings and spent many hours later in his career marrying the two together in his drawings of imaginary landscapes, which in turn were to be echoed in his later castles and their settings.

In spite of their similar training and experience there were differences of temperament between the brothers of the kind that produce a different outlook on work and use of gifts. Thomas Telford made the connection between personality and art in recalling his meeting with the 'affable and communicative' Robert Adam and the 'haughty and reserved' Sir William Chambers in 1782, doing both artists a little less than justice, however:

'a similar distinction of character pervades their works, Sir William's being stiff and formal, those of Mr Adam playful and gay'.[30]

From what we can judge it would not have appealed to the conscientious John Adam to be adventurous in running a prosperous and settled business upon which so many other members of the family, including his own young children, were dependent. His injunction 30 years later to his less responsible brothers, to 'keep to the plain road of their business', had probably always been his creed. Robert, on the other hand, who inherited the creative opportunism of his father on which the prosperity of the Adams had been built, tended to use his resources and every new artistic experience as a springboard from which to take off in his own way, just as he was to form his very personal style from an inventive use of different artistic sources. Admittedly, these characteristics only become clear in the letters from his Italian years and later practice but they cannot have developed overnight. In the urge to make his personal mark he differed from John who seems to have been content to use the designs of others with less adaptation. We cannot tell whether basically different outlooks led to friction between the brothers at this stage in their careers. John's remark years later, after he and Robert had become estranged, that 'there never used to be ceremony between us', suggests a comfortable working relationship on a personal level. Yet the way in which the younger brothers spoke of John in letters ('entre nous autres') suggests that there was a certain distance between them and the head of the family business who was so much their senior. It is also difficult to tell whether Robert found his early work creatively restricting or had hankerings after a wider experience. As a young untrained painter he must have found Paul Sandby's watercolour sketches mature and sophisticated. With regard to architecture, John Clerk's statement that it was as a result of visiting England that Robert 'first began to curb the exuberance of his fancy and polish his taste' is reinforced by the latter's own remark, in February 1755, that 'At London [1749-50] I first felt the change of taste grow on me from that I had contracted in Scotland ...'.[31] Perhaps the unscheduled journey over the Border in the summer of 1752 may have continued to work a change; unfortunately no sketchbook from that journey has survived. His dismissal of Scotland, in the 1750s as a narrow place must surely be a retrospective comment on his early years, so much less exciting than those during which his father had risen to prominence.

James Adam joined the firm only about a year before Robert left home; in 1756 John reminded Robert, who was demanding that James come to Italy before he himself left, 'you know that Jamie's practice and experience is not great'. He feared that his dilletante young brother, his head full of architectural theory, would never learn the practical side of the business at all if allowed at that stage to follow his own inclinations. James had a reputation in the family for being lazy, for which he was rebuked by Robert to whom he occasionally sent unsigned, undated letters or failed to write at all for months at a time. Unlike the energetic Robert, who took to wearing a wig in order to save the valuable business-time taken up in dressing his hair in the mornings, James exasperated Alexander Carlyle during an English holiday because he 'could not get up in the mornings and besides had a very tedious toilette'. He was too young to have benefited from a training by his vigorous father, though he did his duty at Fort George, where he was kept in touch with civilization by long letters from Robert at Rome, and assisted John for at least seven years before leaving on his own Grand Tour in 1760. He was enthusiastic about the theory of architecture and his early drawings, if less credible than Robert's in building terms, are more painterly. His interest in the theory of architecture was encouraged by friends, such as Lord Kames, but an extended essay on the subject begun in Italy was like many of Jamie's projects never finished. He was a loyal partner as long as he had the steadying influence of John or the creative drive of Robert behind him and was able to make his own contribution to the practice.

In the summer of 1754 plans were afoot, at the suggestion of Lord Hopetoun, for Robert to accompany the former's brother, the Hon Charles Hope on a journey to Italy. It was the chance of a lifetime to enlarge his artistic experience, to see at first hand the remains of the ancient world, hitherto familiar in books on architecture or interpreted through the medium of modern buildings, to be able to say he had been in Rome where the greatest practitioners of the art and most deferred-to gentlemen amateurs had spent formative years of their careers, and to gain a whole new, authoritarian dimension for the Adam firm's already considerable reputation at home.

Final confirmation of his plans came while he was at Inveraray in September in the form of a 'vastly civil' letter from Charles Hope in London, then about to embark for Holland, asking Robert to make haste to catch up with him at Paris or, if more convenient, in Holland. It was arranged that James would accompany him as far as France, a considerable sacrifice on the part of the busy John. Having failed to raise letters of introduction for future use from influential acquaintances Robert contented himself with the expectation that Charles Hope's social standing would win him acceptance in the fashionable world. Having arranged to have a seal with his coat-of-arms cut for use on his letters home and promising his sisters to have his portrait painted in Rome he was ready to take a hurried farewell and 'pike off'. A parting glimpse of him in high spirits, in a mood in which he believed nothing could be denied him, has been preserved by Alexander Carlyle whose manse he visited with James and some friends, including John Home, just before leaving:

> 'we found Robert galloping round the green on Piercy [his galloway whom he gave to John Home] like a madman, which he repeated, after seeing us, for at least ten times. Home stopped him, and had some talk with him; so the brothers at last went off quietly for Edinburgh ... Home ... told me what put Robert into such trim. He had been making love to my maid Jenny, who was a handome lass, and had even gone the length of offering to carry her to London, and pension her there. All his offers were rejected, which had put him in a flurry. This happened in summer 1754'.

Robert Adam; miniature on
ivory, attributed to Laurent
Pêcheux, c.1756. Robert
thought his portrait which
Pêcheux painted that year 'as
pretty a little haunty Picture
as I have seen and is worth a
Thousand of Ramsays'; he
also referred to it as 'finished
and now on the chimney piece
before me, .. as resembling as
it is possible for paint to
resemble nature, and vastly
well painted': SRO, Clerk of
Penicuik Muniments,
GD18/4792, 4793.
(Reproduced by permission of
Keith Adam of Blair Adam.
Photograph, Antonia Reeve)

Part two

A KIND OF REVOLUTION

'Sandy', Robert Adam wrote tongue-in-cheek to his friend Alexander MacMillan in 1758, ' ... I know some people through Ignorance of the world and genteel company would call this Self-conceit. But I think it is not amiss for a man to have a little glisk of that Infinite merit he is possess'd of .... You and I are God's begetting'.

It may need a strong stomach for some of the things Bob Adam said about himself in his Italian letters and the remarks he made about other people for that matter. He was not short of self-confidence. 'I hope to make more of being here than any body would imagine', he announced soon after his arrival in Rome in 1755. Over 3 years and a complete change in his own ideas later he was ready to turn his little glisk into a blaze of glory that would outshine all the other stars in the British architectural firmament. He sensed that the time had come for something different and extraordinary. Some of the greatest *cognoscenti* whom he met on his travels assured him, so he said, that he would be 'the remover of taste from Italy to England'. He was determined to outdo rivals such as William Chambers who had had a head-start in the race for English patrons: 'damn my Blood but I will have a fair tryall for it and expect to do as much in Six Months as he has done in as many years'.

As a son of an enterprising and successful father he always had an eye to the main chance and a gift for snatching at the means to his ends, whether the skills of assistants or the synthetic materials and modern methods of manufacture that enabled him to engross the various aspects of his profession. At least one draughtsman was to leave the Adams' London office complaining that he had been made to work like a slave. In a competitive world in which the architectural profession was still not quite sitting comfortably on its august foundations Robert was fully aware of the need to avoid being confused with tradesmen however skilled and specialist. 'It would need a considerable sum every year to appear with proper dignity, keep equippages and establish characters above the common rank of London artificers', he pointed out as he hesitated over the plunge into a London practice.

But there is another Robert Adam inside the ruthlessly ambitious, self-confident young artist and social-climber whom it is so easy to reconstruct from his eminently quotable Italian letters. These must be read in context like any other historical source material. They were, after all, private letters to his immediate family who, like all families, knew the writer in the round, his strengths and weaknesses, and could tell when he was being serious or flippant. His sisters were mainly concerned with his social success, his brothers with his career prospects. It was almost as if he was putting on a performance in writing for their benefit so that they might applaud his triumphs: hobnobbing with cardinals and contessas and adding to his artistic reputation before the eyes of resident artists and travelling connoisseurs. Yet he could reassure his serious-minded sister Betty, 'Don't think, dear Bess, that because I mention these things that I am changed or puffed up with the applause of mankind. God knows that if it were not to divert and amuse you I would never think of it'. With James's premature request for some Roman sketches from which to 'form some idea of a great design' he showed little patience; 'I have not as yet attempted designing anything in the way of composing in the Grand Style as I am applying to those things from which I shall be able to make such compositions ... For I consider beginning compositions just now as one would do a painter who had never learnt to draw hands, feet or eyes and yet would attempt to draw the Laocoon or to compose a history painting'.[32]

However unscrupulous in his determination to come out on top (planning to bring his tutor in Italy, Clérisseau, quietly into Britain after he himself had revealed 'the first flash of character') his integrity as an artist is indisputable. However determined he might be to outdo William Chambers and Robert Mylne he was honest in taking the real measure of his rivals, admitting that he himself had not yet attained the standard and facility in drawing that would fit him for

'My Holy See of Pleasurable Antiquity'. Vignette from a map of Rome, 1748; surveyor, Giambattista Nolli. *(SRO, Register House Plans, 9830)*

the contest. Although he had several years' experience in the family's respected practice behind him when he left home for Europe he was nevertheless prepared to work hard to improve his own style under the influence of the most avant-garde architectural artists of the day. Greatly though he enjoyed the social whirl in Rome's high society he knew that he faced a choice between work and pleasure and for much of the time gave the former priority - although taking care not to let his fashionable acquaintances find him in the street with his sketch-book and pencil. There is much self-assessment in his letters as well as self-esteem. Nor was he always in confident mood; he philosophised on his 28th birthday, 'wambling within me the most green-eyed ideas. But ... heartened myself with thinking how many were older than me and every bit as unsettled and uncertain of their situation and success in life'. By 1758 this doubt had vanished and the great gamble of London lay ahead. For a young man who may long have been feeling for a personal role in the family firm Italy acted as a catalyst opening up the prospect of a very individual contribution to his art. It was the making of Robert Adam.

Barely 3 months after his arrival in Rome and while he was actually visiting Naples in April 1755 Robert received a letter from James suggesting that after his tour he should settle in London instead of returning to Edinburgh. His

Allan Ramsay; self-portrait, gouache, c.1756. After an initial clash of personalities Robert Adam and 'Old Mumpy' became firm friends both in Rome and later. *(Trustees of the National Galleries of Scotland)*

Sir William Chambers; by Sir Joshua Reynolds. Robert Adam's principal professional rival at the height of their careers. *(National Portrait Gallery, London)*

response to an idea which may have been at the back of his mind ever since he first saw London pinpoints not only the practical obstacles in the way of a wider career but just how far he himself felt he had to go before he was ready for it. The least of the problems, as he saw them, was how the Edinburgh firm would manage without him; other Scottish businesses flourished with a partner in London.

> *'It is not that I think Johnie incapable to manage the whole Scotch business, on the Contrary I think him more than Master for it, As he would only have to reject all troublesome and triffling Jobs, & only retain such as would employ his time to purpose & gain Money by advantagious contracts. Thus that difficulty might be overcome ...'.*[33]

A greater problem was what to do about the family, especially if William settled in London, a conjecture 'founded on former conversations', and because 'Scotland is But a narrow place, besides whoever he go's partner with can play their Cards better with a London partner than without'. This would leave James 'the Sole Guardian to so good, so charming a Family'. If James after travelling should 'think of launching out into a greater, a more extensive & more honourable scene, I mean an English Life', the whole family would require to move south, something their Mother would scarcely contemplate at her time of life.

Unlike some of his up-and-coming contemporaries whom he met in Rome Robert was not entirely free to launch out on his own career without resolving existing responsibilities at home. Besides, even with his £5,000 share of the family profits in his bank account when he set out he was not ultimately financially independent but a partner in a firm which was supporting two households. In order to appear professional and distance himself from the 'artificers' in competitive London he would need to be able to call on additional funds. The financial risk was considerable:

> *'If we leave a settled business, a good income, and a cheap country and begin expensively in England, we shall soon spend the little we have made, with uncertainty of success or of making more, ...'.*

The basic reason for his hesitation, however, was more personal and more serious. To succeed in London would require considerable patronage and outstanding merit apart from financial resources. Coming from outside with few influential English contacts it was natural that he should measure his chances against those of potential rivals, such as William Chambers. If, as is usually pointed out, he remained sensitive to rivals and their successes even after he had reached the height of his reputation, it has to be remembered that he had had to make good what he saw as his initial disadvantages largely on his own merits. His efforts were certainly powered by a natural ambition and a very personal attitude to his work. Nevertheless, ambition did not blind him to either his own initial shortcomings or his rival's abilities.

> *'Chambers is a mortal Check to these views in several ways, All the English*

who have travelled for these 5 years are much prepossest in his favours and imagine him a prodigy for Genius, for Sense, & good taste. My own oppinion is that he in good measure deserves their incomium Though his taste is more Architectonick than Pictoresque, ... his taste for Basrelievos, Ornaments and decorations of Buildings, He both knows well & draws exquisitely. His sense is midling, but his appearance is genteel, & his person good which is a most material circumstance. He despises others as much as he admires his own Talents, which he shows with a Slow and dignify'd air, conveying an Idea of great Wisdom, which is no less useful than all his other endowments, and I find sways much with every English man, nay he is in so great esteem ... with most of the English that have been Rome, that they are determin'd to support him to the utmost of their power ...'.

When it came to a comparison of facility in drawing,

'Was I conscious to myself of having Superior Genius of Drawing as well, of being as well provided in good hints for Designing & as many grand designs finish'd finely Drawn & Colour'd as he has to Show away with, it would be a different thing, But that can only come by Time, and Time alone can determine whether I am meet to cope with such a Rival, And if I find that I make the improvement I require, then I can with more certainty trust to English employment & can advise you from time to time if I think I have any prospect of arriving at a Taste much Superior to what I ever though of before I saw Rome, And which at this moment I am quite ignorant of'.[34]

It was a sign of his greater grasp of the standard required that he had to labour to persuade James that he found his genius (personal ability) 'more diminutive since I came abroad than I had before any conception of', so little opportunity had there been at home for comparison.

John Stuart, 3rd Earl of Bute, whose political ascendancy coincided with the early years of Robert Adam's London practice; attributed to Allan Ramsay. *(Trustees of the National Galleries of Scotland)*

Unlike Chambers who had chosen to have a formal art training in Paris which among other things trained the student to be discriminating and selective in what he spent his precious time in Italy studying and copying, Robert found himself almost overwhelmed by the limitless inspiration of the great art gallery and antique-market that was 18th century Rome. Relying on his own good taste and the labours of a band of draughtsmen-recruits, some of whom turned out to have excellent gifts, he set about recording as much as possible in the available time of the construction and ornamentation of surviving classical buildings and their renaissance interpretations, in Rome and its environs and in other Italian locations. It is a tribute to his originality, discrimination and inventiveness that he could later evolve so sophisticated a style from raw material that had been collected at such speed.

He also worked hard at improving his own style of architectural drawing, in which he had the good luck to meet two of the foremost exponents with whom to study. The first was Charles Louis Clérisseau who, having quarrelled with the French Academy in Rome to which he had won a scholarship from Paris, made a living from tutoring artistic hopefuls and selling his paintings of classical ruins to visiting foreigners. The second was the larger-than-life figure of Giovanni Battista Piranesi whose dramatic drawings of surviving classical Rome and powerful imaginary scenes were intended to convey a sense of the power and grandeur of the Roman world (as Piranesi imagined it to have been) rather than an accurate record of its surviving masonry. Robert scarcely achieved the facility and sophistication of Clérisseau's Italian paintings or was aware of the inner life of the great ruins as captured by Piranesi; the latter's 'amazing and ingenious fancies' remained for him 'the greatest fund for inspiring and instilling invention in any lover of architecture that can be imagined'.[35] Contact with these artists had a profound effect on his imagination but it is in his architecture as designed and built rather than in his drawings, that the impact of his Italian experience is seen;

The triumphal South Front of Kedleston Hall, Derbyshire, one of Robert Adam's earliest successes in independent practice. *(Reproduced by permission of the Warburg Institute. Photograph, Royal Commission on the Historical Monuments of England)*

in the ambience of ancient Rome which he could evoke (without academically reproducing it) in the great entrance hall at Syon House, for example, or the marble hall at Kedleston.

Although planning his prospects in hardheaded fashion, Robert remained 'a picturesque hero' at heart, equally enthusiastic in his letters about the living Italian landscape as about the remains of its ancient buildings:

> *'All the rarie shows finished on Tuesday night and on Wednesday Clérisseau and I sallied forth into the country and walked seven or eight miles to digest the fatigues of the carnival in the beauties of natural objects masked to none who have taste or genius to view them out, views and landscapes more enchanting than ever. In short, my dear ladies, this is the most intoxicating country in the world for a picturesque hero'.*

He also took enthusiastically to the pursuits of the antiquarian, 'or as we say in Scotland an Antick'. By the time he left Rome his lodgings in the Casa Guarnieri were full of his collection of paintings, drawings, casts from the antique and actual fragments of antiquity. Some of his happiest hours were spent in galleries and salerooms or in fulfilling commissions to buy paintings, including some for the Earl of Hopetoun and Robert Dundas of Arniston. His enjoyment of books and portfolios of drawings and engravings must have contributed to the pleasure he obviously took in designing clients' libraries. James's great scoop, while in Italy in his turn, in purchasing Cardinal Albani's fine collection of drawings for King George III could scarcely have happened without the influence of Robert who had been on visiting terms in the Cardinal's galleries. In November 1756 he heard from John of the death of the family's old friend and patron, Sir John Clerk of Penicuik:

> *'Baron Clerk he tells me is even defunct at last and the whole Town in Mourning for his old Body. I began to count Kindred, at which the Lord and you all know I am not a dab, to find if I ought to lay aside my Blue and Silver Suit and lament over the old Antiquarian in Sack Cloath and Ashes. It's a pity the Bod defuncked before he saw some of my Antique Collection of Curiositys. I am sure it would have revived the Saul of him for half a Dozen years longer'.*

The publication of a work on Antiquity was a prestigious way in which to make one's name in knowledgeable circles. Robert's scheme for a projected book on the Baths of Diocletian and Caracalla did not materialise nor did his plans to produce a revised edition of Desgodetz's *Ancient Buildings of Rome*, with which he found many faults when comparing it with the originals. He was, however, 'determined, in imitation of Scotch heroes [of his acquaintance] to become an author, to attack Vitruvius, Palladio and those blackguards of ancient and modern architecture, sword in hand'. His greatest project to reach fruition was the volume of drawings of *The Remains of the Emperor Diocletian's Palace at Spalatro* (modern Split in Croatia) for which the drawings were done on the site by his stalwart band of draughtsmen led by Clérisseau. In one respect it failed as the promotional publication it was meant to be. By the time the handsome, specially-bound copy was presented to the royal dedicatee, George III, in 1764 Robert's London practice had taken off; he had upstaged himself.

It was an undoubted advantage to make the most of his introduction to the high society of Rome procured for him on the credit of the Honourable Charles Hope's social standing. Yet time spent on pleasure was time lost in study. 'Shall I lose Hope and my introduction to the great, or shall I lose Clérisseau and my taste for the grand?' - a considerable dilemma. On the one hand, with his sociable nature, sense of fun and enjoyment of music and dancing Robert was having the time of his life: singing after supper to 'the Italians who are vastly diverted with the sound their airs have from a foreign mouth'; attending the Opera where he listened 'not without a Certain feeling of Transport I never felt before'; dancing at fashionable gatherings where 'I had seasoned myself pretty well by at least 50 minuets each night'; driving his little second-hand green calash round the streets of Rome, 'by which means I have acquired an immense dexterity in a very short time, and believe few Roman charioteers ever turn'd the Goal with more address and Celerity'; and throwing himself into all the 'Madness and Distraction' of the Carnival where, disguised as Pulcinello, he pranced from room to room at the elbow of that most sociable of clerics, Abbé Peter Grant, who 'took everybody by the sleeve who had a black domino with red ribbons, calling him Mr Adams and swearing it was strange what had become of me'.

Fun was fun, but socialising for its own sake eventually bored him unless it held out the promise of an introduction to a potential patron or an invitation to a private art collection; 'really, the only thing one could wish to see these people for is to say you have seen them, in case you should be looked down upon by your own countrymen'. While Robert's self-esteem helped him to keep his end up in the noblest company, the fashionable James seems to have felt the incongruity of hobnobbing with the patricians of Rome more keenly.

After Robert and Charles Hope drifted apart, the acrimony diplomatically concealed in public but poured out in Robert's letters to his family, he was free to make his own friends and invite them to his comfortable if cluttered lodgings-cum-studio in the Casa Guarnieri where he and Clérisseau lived and worked amicably. He chose a house in a fashionable part of the city rather than in the artists' quarter. He was also careful to portray himself outwardly in the role of patron of his artistic mentors, Clérisseau and the Frenchman Pêcheux, who painted his portrait, but they were in fact his teachers, captured on the rebound from tutoring Chambers among others. His relationship with Allan Ramsay, an earlier Edinburgh friend, who by the 1750s was an established artist on his second visit to Italy, took longer to settle down but after an initial clash of temperaments they became firm friends with a respect for each other's gifts. Allan encouraged Robert to try his luck in London. Mrs Ramsay was a good friend from the start:

'I am sure poor Mrs Ramsay is to be pitied spending her life in a dreary way in this place. Though she is of so good a family, her being the wife to an artist prevents her being admitted into any company ... Allan is a caput tyrannical body in his own house'.

What he evidently enjoyed most was the freedom, 'unmolested by Kirk or State', 'to take my book and go wherever I please'; it was a charmed if hectic life.

'I am returned to my studies', he announced after the Carnival, 'to feast on marble ladies, to dance attendance in the chamber of Venus and to trip a minuet with Old Otho, old Cicero and those other Roman worthies whose very busts seem to grin contempt at my legerity. Now I spend the night among virtuosis and their works ... Now and then I launch out into the finer world and again I retire among my worthy fellow connoisseurs ... In one hour I doat upon my Marquis Corsi, next you see me among a heap of portfolios'.

He felt most at ease with fellow-Scots, his 'Caledonian Club' as he called them; Abbé Peter Grant ('Dear Old Grantibus') who could fix up anything for a traveller, from decent lodgings to an introduction to a Cardinal, Mr and Mrs Elliot, she a 'good-natured, clever little woman', he 'a most insignificant, trifling mortal' whose only interest was in 'Genteelity', Gavin Hamilton the painter and the Ramsays. 'A man will always be merriest speaking his native language and cracking his jokes in his ain Mither tongue', as he no doubt did with the old Jacobite, Dr Irvine, who had preserved his native Scots tongue 'pure and undefiled' although 'he has not seen the Land of Cakes since the battle of Sheriffmuir'. On a momentous St Andrew's Night he attended a supper given by the Earls of Rosebery and Elgin, at which he got so 'beastly drunk' that he had to be carried home where he was put to bed by Clérisseau, his own manservant Donald being in a similar state and 'unfit to perform that office'.

Only his artistic preoccupations saved him, so he claimed, from falling in love. Allusions in his letters hint at one or two passing attachments before he left home, apart from the maid at Inveresk manse, and when writing to James (with whom, so he said, he shared a dislike of the bonds of matrimony) he sent occasional teasing greetings to 'Heiress Whyte', daughter of the clerk Alexander White, threatening to come home and marry her 'and raise up many Storys of Rubbled headed Boys and polish'd Ashler faced Girls'. He obviously enjoyed the company of the women whom he met in Italy, to the most handsome of whom he would give a 'twirl' in his green chariot, and once laid himself up for two days with an injury got by falling over a friend's trunk as he 'marched briskly' through his lodging in the dark in search of the landlady's daughter, 'a very pretty girl'. The woman who made most impression on him in Italy, Miss Diana Molyneux, a lady of good English family who was travelling with her sick sister, Mrs Berry, was some years his senior, well-read and a sympathetic admirer of his work. Her coquettish reaction to his cocksureness had caused a clash of personalities on their first meeting but he later became a frequent visitor to her household:

'I must say for her', he admitted, 'I never saw so agreeable a woman or so accomplished, with an inexhaustible fund of good sense, a most pleasing address and engaging manner ... If my heart was not as hard as iron I would undoubtedly be head over ears and desperation in love. But, thank God, my plans and elevations and Baths and virtu have a surprising effect to keep down

that passion'. When she came to breakfast to see his drawings, she exclaimed, *'"Lord Bless me, is it possible that that gay, cheerful and frolicsome Mr Adams that we see at our house is the same studious, laborious and enterprising Mr Adams that we see at his own? I am surprised how you can laugh, how you can joke and be merry when you have such a crowd of objects and ideas to distract your imagination ... The twentieth part would turn my brain"'*.

By the autumn of 1755 the doubts about his own readiness for a London career were beginning to evaporate under Clérisseau's tuition and Piranesi's inspiration, and as his collection of artistic capital increased until one of the rooms in his lodging was 'as full as it can stick' of casts, mouldings, antique ornaments and portfolios of drawings, either purchased or done by himself and his draughtsmen. Looking to the future needs of a London office, he may already have seen the need to train James as his partner, not to mention his brother's immediate usefulness in completing his ambitious survey of Roman buildings. On 19 October he wrote to James (the letter being sent under cover to John McGowan to keep it from the rest of the family) asking his younger brother to join him in Rome as soon as possible. The ensuing correspondence reveals the attitudes of William Adam's 'promising young men' at this important juncture in their careers. 'Unless Something unforeseen makes my friends advise and myself think of returning to Scotland, you may reckon me Settled in England', Robert announced and demanded to know the reason for his brothers' delay in settling which of them should travel next. He suspected that John was holding back until Robert, with two more years in Italy behind him, was ready to hold the fort in Edinburgh while John himself went abroad. That would set back by four years (allowing John a two-year tour) Robert's settling in London. It would also mean that Clérisseau would have gone home leaving John without an adviser in Rome, a pointless exercise. In fact, Robert had begun to wonder what John would get out of the experience:

'... *when he is in Rome he cannot propose Studying in the extensive way, as he does not know much of Landscape, of Figures or Perspective, without which he could not better himself much of what he sees of the Ancient Remains by making Views of them ...'*.

He tried to picture his older brother,

'*studying from the beginning. Drawing things in the street & labouring at Feet, hands & Bodys for 3/4th of a Year, so that all he can reap is the improvement in seeing & measuring the Geometrical plans and Elevations, & the great advantage of having it to say one was in Italy'*.[36]

James, on the other hand, he insisted, was just the right age and he urged him to set out for Italy now, when all advantages were available, including Clérisseau as tutor. If the idea did not appeal to James he should destroy the letter, if it did, 'Then you may Take what course you think propperest to discover it to your friends?

'Not a little surpris'd' at the contents, James showed the letter to John 'as the person most interested in the Scheme and whose advice I wou'd soonest follow'. John, 'with the utmost ease' told James he must please himself whether he went or not, but advised him to wait a bit longer. Whatever John thought of Robert's assessment of his own abilities and prospects, he did not choose to comment on it beyond saying that he had read the letter over 'several times, & considered, so much as a Crowd of Ideas flocking into one's mind at the same time will admitt off'. John Adam's lot was the mixed blessing of being the oldest son. Many an heir, be it to a business or a barony, had to carry the burden of setting his siblings up in life from the family patrimony, which was what John did. Writing to Robert in January 1756 on the business of James's study-tour, after it had been postponed to Robert's great disappointment, John vowed:

'I made no hesitation to his going as I never shall stand in the way of people so nearly connected by blood and friendship doing whatever shall appear most for their advantage'.

It was not that he felt unable to carry on the business alone, he had done so already when his brothers had departed together on the first stage of Robert's journey.

'But I think the loss must evidently have been [James's] by being called off from his application to the study of the practice to that of the theory before he was well rooted. You know Jamie's practice and experience is not great and that he would immediately forget it upon his turning his mind entirely to the theory at Rome'.[37]

Robert may have felt differently, to judge from a letter which he wrote to Lord Kames in 1763 in the midst of his own busy practice:

'My Brother James writes with that love and Enthusiasm of Architecture which no one could feel that has not formed very extensive ideas of it. It is easy to tame and bring under proper management those large Views, and the Detail of our profession comes naturally. But the architect who begins with the Minutae, will never Rise above the Race of these Reptile Architects who have Infested and Craul'd about this country for these many years'.[38]

To Robert, 'extensive ideas' were essential in making the kind of impact he hoped for, and he was probably prepared to remedy James's inexperience by keeping him hard at work once they were together, so long as he could harness his enthusiasm. Think big and the rest will follow, is what he seems to be saying to Kames, but begin with 'minutae' and you will always have a reptile's eye view of the profession. Practice must serve the theory. He would have endorsed the opinion of the musician Sir Peter Pears who once said, 'Technique is the liberation of imagination'.

In the end James decided to wait rather than curtail his sightseeing en route to Rome or delay his joining Robert in London while John visited Italy. He spent longer abroad than Robert in the end but accomplished less, except for capturing the Albani drawings and handling the Italian end of the production of *Spalatro*. Passages from his long unfinished essay on Architecture are echoed in *The Works in Architecture of Robert and James Adam* (1773) but his projected volume on the 'Antiquities of Sicily and Grecia Major' was abandoned, as well as several expeditions including his plans to visit Greece.

John's prospects of visiting Italy gradually faded. He must have had private doubts about leaving James in charge, although he did envisage this, and he must have considered it a waste of investment if Robert, having decided to settle in London, did not do so immediately upon his return; in fact, he advised Robert to do precisely that when writing to him in January 1756 about James's plans. The following July Robert was asking James why John still hesitated; 'My opinion is he never will [travel] & in that resolution I leave him and go to plan our Schemes [for London]'. Yet the idea was kept afloat in correspondence. In November 1756 Robert, in a letter to John, defended his dismissal of William Kent's garden designs by saying, 'when you have known your fellow-traveller-to-be [Clérisseau] as long as I have you will have no difficulty in joining in my assertion'. The following spring, however, his old patron Lord Dumfries, dashed John's hopes by reacting strongly to the idea of his architect's going abroad. Writing to James from the Earl's house, Leiffnorris, on 14 May 1757, John related how, having found Lord Dumfries in a good humour, he told him about Robert's intention of settling in London; 'he wish'd him well wherever he was'. When John then divulged his own travel plans, however,

> 'you cannot conceive how much he was confounded ... and said that appeared to him most extraordinary, that we should undertake people's work & then go One by One & leave it. That for his part he was an ignorant man in all these matters & I must be sensible it was to me he had trusted, as both my Brothers were young when he begun, and that it was in my experience he trusted still, so that it was a thing he could by no means consent to'.

No amount of reassurance, that James would attend the work assiduously, that the drawings were finished and the moulds ready did any good;

> 'it was beating the Air to say anything to him. He was deaf and inexorable, so that I was obliged to promise him that at present I should not go. This is a most damnable dilemma, and tho' I am very much concerned at my own disappointment yet your Situation gives me much more pain ... I am not sure but it would be as well for you to remain a little longer here for the sake of practice, which I think is of consequence to one in his theory'.[39]

The incident underlines just how clearly a patron might regard his architect as a retained, if skilled, official at his personal disposal. The following day the normally sober John finished his letter at Kilmarnock, 'with a very sore head, having been oblig'd to exceed a little last night as it was the last' with Lord Dumfries. It must have been difficult to be convivial after such a blow to his hopes. He did not go to Italy. No doubt he would have enjoyed the personal encounter with the tangible remains of the ancient world which, as much as Robert, he had been brought up to revere. In spite of their different temperaments and outlook there is no indication that John resented the way in which Robert's particular gifts made room for themselves in the family practice or the success that came to him as a result of capitalising on his Italian experience, so long as he acted prudently. Whether or not there is evidence of Robert's design-ability before leaving Scotland, it was recognised by John who turned to his brother in that capacity from time to time, even in matters of such personal interest to himself as a projected book of garden designs or the proposed transformation of his beloved Blair House. It was the way Robert went about things that John sometimes found fault with: taking opposition head-on, continually glancing over his shoulder at rivals, like a front-runner in a race, and doggedly demanding compensation for every injury, whether to his pride or his pocket, while himself taking money matters lightly.

Robert, facing the expense of the London gamble wanted his partnership with John to continue indefinitely, 'by which means the first outfitting would not be so heavy on the beginner', hoping that the initial outlay would later be made good. John agreed to continue the partnership for a year after Robert's return. As things turned out they were not to be financially independent of each other for long. Robert arrived in London just after New Year 1758: 'my dearest Mother's British boy'.

'The Man of Taste' caricatured by Hogarth.

ABOVE *the* COMMON RANK

*L*ike his programme of artistic self-improvement in Italy Robert Adam's setting-up in London in 1758 was hard work to start with, in many ways much harder. Whereas his studies had been pursued privately in his lodgings or in the company of friends, his bid to establish himself professionally in the competitive metropolis was a public affair requiring all his reserves of self-confidence and powers of persuasion. Introductions had to be sought and clients captured. His house was fitted up like a modern designer's showroom, to evoke the ambience of the classical world and all those adjuncts to a civilised patron's lifestyle. Potential clients could judge the architect's ability and taste from his own drawings done on the spot in Italy, his collection of the drawings of others, discriminating selection of old masters' and modern paintings and display of antique sculptural fragments and carvings. He had to convince his visitors that he knew how to use his artistic repertoire imaginatively and that their own bespoke designs would be new and individual. 'With his taste and productions and manners everyone went away enchanted', wrote John Clerk fulsomely, no doubt referring to what James described as 'the long London mornings when Bob used to hold forth to his company, at the expense of much time and many words'. It was not a profession for the fainthearted.

James stayed with Robert in London for 3 months early in 1758 in his furnished lodgings in Cleveland Court no doubt giving his brother moral support as he trudged with his drawings from one great man's house to another's, kicking his heels in their anterooms and 'putting on a face of brass' as a self-appointed salesman, for that, essentially, was what he was. A few requests for designs came in while James was still with him, who reassured the family in Edinburgh that 'small things begin already to cast up and large, I hope, will follow soon'. The early months were cheered by the reconstitution of the circle of 'good Edinburgh companions', who were either immigrants to London like himself or there on business: John Home, now secretary to the ascendant Earl of Bute, William Robertson, in the city about the publication of his *History of Scotland*, Alexander Carlyle for his sister's wedding, Robert's old friend Adam Ferguson, then a private tutor, Alexander Wedderburn and Jack Dalrymple. The friends dined together every Wednesday in a coffee house in Savile Row, rounding off the evening with a visit to Drury Lane Theatre where they watched David Garrick who was to prove a good friend to the Adams.

Before long Robert improved his circumstances by moving into a house of his own in Lower Grosvenor Street, bought with a loan from John of £1,400. The loan was only one aspect of the strain which the London office began to put on the family resources. Two sisters, Jenny and Betty, moved south to take on what Robert called his 'Domestick determinations' and William, leaving the office of Adam Fairholm in Edinburgh where he had trained, came to keep the books. Robert, although he had been fascinated by mathematics at university and explored the creative possibilities of the science in his designs, nevertheless loathed the practical business of book-keeping.

> *'Accounts will be a Plague'*, he had written to James when contemplating the London venture, *'I often wish for John's Arithmetical head & Sanders Whyte swelled thumb to keep my legers in order. If it please the Most High in heaven and those on Earth to give me Subject matter for those perplexing Folios I wish you would think a thousand times on this subject .... considering my ignorance & abhorrence of all Maner of Calculations'.*[40]

As the time drew near for James's departure Robert sent to Edinburgh drawings of classical ornament to copy in order to 'fix the antique manner in your head', and asked for John's gifted young draughtsman George Richardson to be sent to London for more sophisticated training prior to his accompanying James to Europe. Clearly, if it was Robert's dream, as he once expressed it, that 'the Adams be the sovereign Architects of the United Kingdom' the Edinburgh establishment rather than that of 'the beginner' in London looked like becoming the branch office.

David Garrick (1717-1779) actor and theatre manager, friend and neighbour of the Adams in the Adelphi, for whom Robert re-designed the Drury Lane Theatre in 1775-6. 'Why, now', he once remarked, 'the Adams are as liberal-minded men as any in the world: but I don't know how it is, all their workmen are Scotch'. Drawn by N Dance *(National Portrait Gallery, London)*

The most important contacts of the first two years were made through the interest of the small but influential circle of fellow-Scots in what the homesick William dubbed 'this Roast Beef society' of upper-class London. Gilbert Elliot, John's old schoolfellow, now through the Argyll interest MP for Selkirkshire and a Lord of the Admiralty, gained for Robert his first public commission, the screen wall to the Admiralty building in Whitehall. Robert may have pinned great hopes on the effect of this 'first flash of character', standing as it did in full view of the government men, but public commissions were to prove illusive. The aged 3rd Duke of Argyll, builder of Inveraray, extended hospitality and arranged for possible clients to visit Lower Grosvenor Street but failed to produce the public appointment Robert wanted to confirm his standing. Lord Hope, the Earl of Hopetoun's heir, introduced him to Lord Mansfield, the Scots-born Lord Chief Justice, whose friendship he retained for life, although it was 1764 before the first drawings were made for Kenwood House, Hampstead, which Lord Mansfield had bought from the Earl of Bute 10 years before.

Robert's first attempt to attract the attention of Bute himself, who was in the confidence of the Prince of Wales before his accession as George III in 1760, was something of a humiliation. When he and some friends were introduced by Bute's secretary, John Home, they were received by the great man 'booted and spurred', were not asked to sit down and very soon took their leave.

'No sooner were we out of hearing', Alexander Carlyle recalled, *'than Robert Adam ... fell a-cursing and swearing. "What ! had he been presented to all the princes in Italy and France, and most graciously received, to come and be treated with such distance and pride by the youngest earl but one in Scotland?" They were better friends afterwards and Robert found him a kind patron, when his professional merit was made known to him'.*[41]

William Murray, 1st Earl of Mansfield, Lord Chief Justice; by David Martin. Lord Mansfield, for whom Robert Adam designed Kenwood House, remained an influential friend. *(Trustees of the National Galleries of Scotland)*

In 1762 Bute commissioned him to revise plans (prepared by Brettingham) for a site on the corner of Berkley Square, usually known as Lansdowne House, which after Bute's fall from power he completed for Lord Shelburne who bought the house on the recommendation of his adviser and friend of the Adams, General Robert Clerk. By then he was also remodelling and designing interiors for Shelburne's country house at Bowood in Wiltshire.

It was to two other Scots, Lady Lindores and General Lord Charles Hay, younger brother of William Adam's patron the Marquess of Tweeddale, that he owed his introduction to his first major country house clients, Edwin Lascelles of Gawthorpe and Harewood, Yorkshire, and Sir Nathaniel Curzon of Kedleston in Derbyshire. In both cases the client had already engaged another architect, John Carr at Harewood and Matthew Brettingham, elder, and James Paine at Kedleston. As a result these commissions were for the alteration and completion of the buildings and the design and decoration of the interiors.

Nevertheless he did put his stamp on these two magnificent country houses.

The Library at Kenwood House, Hampstead. *(Country Life)*

Externally, his alterations to Carr's design for Harewood were restrained since the plan did not 'admit of a great many alterations' but James congratulated him on having 'tickled it up so as to dazzle the eyes of the squire'. Internally, where the decoration and furnishing extended over the first decade of his practice, he had a freer hand, although the careful patron warned his sanguine young architect, 'Let us do everything properly and well, *mais pas trop*'. The triumphal south front and splendid marble hall at Kedleston were designed while the impressions of the grandeur of Rome and the contact with artists such as Piranesi were still fresh in Robert's mind. The excitement accompanying the turn-up at Kedleston is conveyed in his letters to James, then in Italy. Sir Nathaniel was 'struck all of a heap' with Robert's drawings:

'... *every new drawing he saw made him grieve at his previous engagement with Brettingham. He carried me home in his chariot about three o'clock and kept me to four o'clock seeing all said Brettingham's designs and asked my opinion. I proposed alterations and desired he might call them his own fan-*

Design for the ceiling for the hall at Cullen House, Banffshire; Robert Adam, 1767. (SRO, *Register House Plans*, 2542/4)

Ceiling for the Hall at Cullen House.

cies ... I revised all his plans and got the entire management of his grounds ... with full powers as to temples, bridges, seats and cascades, so that as it is seven miles round you may guess the play of genius and scope for invention ...'.[42]

On 24 July 1760 he reported, in high spirits:

'We have had the greatest revolutions at Sir Nat's that ever you heard of ... And now none of them setts a stone or Cutts a bitt of Timber without my Positive instructions, which occasions my writing at least 3 or 4 letters every week and drawing sketches, moulds, etc, eternally. I have got the Design of his Bridge over the fall of water finished which looks magnificent & I am convinced Cle[risseau] would even approve of. Allons, Allons, allez votre train, O ho! ... bravo! bravo!'.

He was less elated about his solitary public commission so far:

'The wall of the Admiralty advances slowly. But if once the Board of Works were done with us we shall soon make a figure. They have taken as much time to turn a drain that carrys the Water from the River to St James's Park as they might have pulled down & rebuilt the whole Admiralty'.[43]

On 31 March 1763 he apologised to Lord Kames:

Monument to the botanist Sir Charles Linnaeus, designed by Robert Adam (1778) and erected by Dr John Hope. It now stands in the Royal Botanic Gardens, Edinburgh. *(Royal Commission on the Ancient and Historical Monuments of Scotland)*

'I am ashamed to say I have had the honour of your letter of the 2nd ultimo so long without its being in my power to answer it sooner. The practice of Architecture rushes so fast upon me that I have but too few moments to dedicate to Theory and Speculation ... I have been twice in the Country Since I received your Lordships Letter & if I may judge by my own employment private Buildings go on apace. I expect to be very litle in London all this Summer, Having business all over England, which I am with difficulty able to get managed with Honour to myself and satisfaction to my Employers'.[44]

The success of his practice was underwritten by the labours of a highly skilled team of draughtsmen and decorative artists some of whom he had recruited in Italy, so much so that some of their critics accused the Adams of having risen to prominence 'on the backs of the Italians'. In the firm's first decade the draughtsmen included Laurent-Benôit Dewez and Agostino Brunias, who had both been on the expedition to Spalatro, and the Scot, George Richardson, who returned from Italy with his own knowledge of architecture transformed and was eventually to leave behind him a list of publications that would have been the envy of James Adam who had treated him rather high-handedly during their travels. The decorative paintings which formed an integral part of Adam interior design, particularly of ceiling designs, were executed by Antonio Zucchi and Angelica

Kedleston Hall, Derbyshire, entrance hall, view to the south; Robert Adam *(Royal Commission on the Historical Monuments of England)*

Kauffmann, who became husband and wife and departed for Italy in 1781, Giovanni Battista Cipriani who was given the important early commission to decorate the ceiling of the drawing room at Syon, Biagio Rebecca, and Michelangelo Pergolesi whose book of *Designs for Various Ornaments* (published 1777-1801) helped to disseminate the decorative style of the Adam office. The scale and distinction of the firm's work helped to prosper the careers of a number of specialist collaborators, such as Joseph Rose, the distinguished plasterer, with his nephew and namesake, John Linnell the furniture maker and Matthew Boulton who produced high quality metal goods and is believed to have made the elegant lamps that hang on the staircase at Osterley Park. All kinds of manufacturers were eventually to feel what Sir John Soane called 'the electric power of this Revolution in Art'.

Heveningham Hall, Suffolk, entrance hall, view to the West; James Wyatt, who most clearly rivalled the Adams in their own style. *(Royal Commission on the Historical Monuments of England)*

By the time James joined him in London towards the end of 1763 Robert had designed and in many cases partly or entirely built some of those early commissions which most clearly demonstrate his individual style, including the extension to a house at Islesworth for General Humphry Bland, Governor of Edinburgh Castle, where the edge was taken off his satisfaction with this first private commission by the 'angly, stiff sharp manner' of the English plasterers; Hatchlands in Surrey for Admiral Boscawen, another contact through Gilbert Elliot; Shardeloes, Buckinghamshire, for William Drake; Kedleston and Harewood, Croome Court, Worcestershire, for the Earl of Coventry, Mersham Hatch in Kent for Sir Wyndham Knatchbull; as well as the early phases of the most prestigious commission of them all, the magnificent Roman palace at Syon, Middlesex, for the Duke of Northumberland, where Robert remodelled the interior of the existing Jacobean House; and the beginnings of the modernisation of the Elizabethan house at Osterley Park, Middlesex, for the banker, Robert Child, where the survival of the decoration and furniture illustrates the whole range of the artist's style over 20 years.

The creation and direction of all this work was accomplished by Robert himself before James came home, 'with difficulty', perhaps, as he admitted to Lord Kames but to the great credit, nevertheless, of his powers of invention and capacity for work. 'I believe he can draw plans faster than I can draw cornishes', declared James who was to ride on the crest of a wave with his brother almost to the end of the decade during which Robert experienced his father's success of nearly 40 years earlier, but at an even faster pace. The euphoria of these first few years is captured in Betty Adam's letters to James in Italy:

'Townshend's Monument is now putting up in the [Westminster] abby & will very soon be finish'd ... Carter, the man who puts it up askd Brittingham, who came to look at it, what was really his opinion of it. "Why really ... I think there is nothing equal to it in the Abbey", which was really good from a Man that had been supplanted by Bob more than once ...'.[45]

'Bob returned from Beckfords on thursday after fixing the ground for the situation of his house & prevailing with him to have as much patience as delay the laying the foundation till the Design was ready, which was not then begun. He is gone out today with Lord Northumberland to Sion, has dined there & is not yet returned. My lords good opinion of him seems to increase the more he sees of him & I dare say that will always be the case where he has to do with people of taste'.[46]

In 1761 James reported in turn, from Italy:

'Johny writes me a long letter in which he mentions with great satisfaction Bob's present prospect of success & his good luck in the concurring circumstances ... I make not the smallest doubt that his Joy is sincere ...'.[47]

Although the great period of 18th-century country house building was over Robert had taken another tide at the flood, that of a change of mood in public taste. This was largely to be found among non-aristocratic newly-rich patrons who were ready for something new, free from the static architectural conventions and the predictable use of forms by the Palladian school, the interiors of whose houses, however grand, would be decidedly domestic rather than public in character. Robert Adam's individual interpretation of the antique, the apparently endless variation in his use of classical forms and motifs, however much it might offend the purists, was welcomed by this new clientèle. Besides which, the accession of a young King in 1760, who was known to be a lover of the arts, seemed to augur well for the public encouragement of the arts and artistic institutions.

As the most fashionable London-based architect, with a growing practice that sent him 'almost constantly wandering from county to County', as he put it to Mrs Montague in 1766, Robert was at his furthest from Scotland in this decade. The designs that issued from his office, imbued with the effects of his direct encounter with the remains of antiquity, seem worlds away from the kind of work which he had helped to execute at home in the early 1750s. No less than the revolution in his art, the extent to which he demonstrated his ability to control quality, deploy the skills of others and keep on top of a competitive profession shows how far he had travelled in less than a decade from the 'very clever lad' who had been junior partner to John in the Edinburgh office.

Most Scots patrons in the 1760s were the London-Scots for whom work was done in town and country, the most prestigious of which being the remodelling of Kenwood House for Lord Mansfield where the library with its vaulted ceiling and apsidal ends beyond screens of Corinthian columns remains one of Robert's finest interiors. There was also Luton Park, the Earl of Bute's mansion in Bedfordshire, the exterior of which, as the architect pointed out, was treated almost as in a public rather than private building, although by the time it began to be built (1766) it commemorated rather than advertised Bute's position since he had by then fallen from power; it remained unfinished until after Robert Adam's death. Some external additions were made to Moor Park, Hertfordshire, for Sir Lawrence Dundas besides alterations, decoration and furniture for his London house in Arlington Street. There was also Fife House in Whitehall for the Earl of Fife, and interior decoration at the Earl of Eglinton's house in Piccadilly. At the very end of the decade he began to plan the layout of the Bathwick estate, Bath, for William Johnston, who changed his name to Pulteney on his marriage to the heiress to the estate, for whose family, the Johnstons, Robert was to carry out several commissions spanning his whole career.

Those few fellow-countrymen who asked him for plans for their Scottish residences in the 1760s had close personal or family connections with the south. Perhaps because of the unlikelihood of his personal supervision and the probability of a local architect-builder's taking over the work, Robert may have relied less on his personal repertoire and more on the pattern-books than he would have done for a contemporary southern client. At any rate it has been pointed out that the floor plans for Moy House which he drew up in 1759 for Sir Ludovic Grant were adapted from *The Modern Builder's Assistant*, as were some elements of the interiors for his early Scottish country house, Auchincruive, Ayrshire, begun in 1766 for Richard Oswald, government agent and contractor and plantation owner, who had recently acquired the property. The hall and dining-room ceilings at Auchincruive, with their naturalistic motifs, seem to echo the character of the Brothers' early Scottish work rather than the geometric elements of Robert's contemporary English ceilings, although the entwined thyrsus and ivy also appear in his early work at Shardeloes. The ceilings which Robert and James designed in the 1760s for Cullen House, which were not executed, more clearly show the characteristics of those being designed for English clients. The difficulties of executing the work when both the architect and the owner were in far-off London is illustrated in the letters sent to Richard Oswald of Auchincruive by his factor:

'*The Chaff House to be made a Malting House and a Kill [Kiln]. To be built as high as the midle Stable if no material objection from Mr Adams*'.

'*The whole work in your New house Goes on very slowly and in Short I have no pleasure in looking at what is done ... I do wish & intreat that you could find some more able person to direct and conduct the execution of the work in the principall story, so that you may have some comfort in the possessing of it, the ornaments that are made look in generall very heavie & are not clean done ...*'.[48]

An estimate of the cost of a modest house 'to be built at Elgin, contracted by Andrew Smith', undated and for an unknown client but endorsed '1766', was prepared 'from a plan sent from London by Messrs Adams'. The document's survival in the Seafield Muniments almost certainly suggests that the client was a relative of that family.[49]

About 1762, in the heady days of his first English successes, Robert was approached by the Royal College of Physicians of Edinburgh for his opinion on a plan which they had had prepared for a new Hall for their premises. Tempting his clients with more than they asked for, he offered them a plan for a Hall and Library estimated to cost between £5-6000 to build. To his disappointment the College declined. A few years later the physicians were obliged to relinquish a plan to build on the site earmarked for his Register House.[50] The opportunity to design a large public building in Edinburgh, albeit a severely functional one, came in 1763 when the Trustees of the 'Royal Academy for Teaching Excercises' (or Riding School) instructed John Fordyce 'to write to Mr Adam at London to consult with Sir Sydney Meadows and Mr Bellinger concerning a plan'. The first Governor of the Academy was the Earl of Bute and the Trustees included some Adam clients, present and to come, such as Sir Laurence Dundas, Mure of Caldwell and the Duke of Buccleuch. Making the most of this public commission Robert not only forwarded drawings about 6 weeks later but offered to make out a fuller plan for 'the extension of our scheme, and forming a complete academy for fencing, dancing, etc and having houses for the different masters, all formed on a regular plan; making the Riding House the centre building'. This gentlemanly institution, which may never have been completed to the Adam plan, was a functional Palladian building with only sufficient ornament 'to make the facade decent and genteel'. It did not have a very long life as an Academy and the building itself was demolished in 1870.[51]

Of more significance was Robert Adam's connection, through Edinburgh artistic and antiquarian friends, with the Board of Manufactures' School of Design, an association which he established in the 1760s and which lasted for over 20 years, during which he was asked, with other London mentors, for advice in appointing masters for the schools and maintaining an acceptable standard in the students' work. David Allan, the painter, was appointed on the suggestion of Robert Adam and Robert Strange, the engraver. This element of consultancy also crops up in occasional private Scottish contacts. In the case of the new Penicuik House, Midlothian, built by the son of William Adam's old patron, the exchange of ideas with the gentleman-amateur architect, Sir James Clerk, ended in the latter's rejection of Robert's dismissive comments on his plans, in spite of the mediation of General Robert Clerk; 'tho' I should give 20 guineas for his consultation', the General told Sir James, 'I give it with pleasure for I would give a hundred guineas rather than you have an improper house'.

The decade which saw Robert firmly established in his London practice found John with sole responsibility for what turned out to be the last full decade of his own practice north of the Border. His work, which awaits detailed study, included commissions all over the country; his surviving letters to clients often refer to his journeys. Private work included the completion of Douglas Castle, Lanarkshire, for the Duke of Douglas (1761); that of several smaller works at Inveraray for the Duke of Argyll (1760-1); Ballochmyle House, Ayrshire, for Allan Whitefoord (c.1760); a library at the Whim, Peeblesshire, also for Argyll (1761); Moffat House, for Lord Hopetoun (1761); Balnagowan, for Captain John Ross (plan accepted, January 1762); offices for Kerse House, Stirlingshire, for Robert Adam's client, Sir Laurence Dundas (1763); continued work at Castle Grant (1763-5); stables at Dunrobin for the Earl of Sutherland (1766) and the remodelling of Broomhall, Fife, for the Earl of Elgin, which went on until 1771.

In the field of public works (apart from his government contracts) he failed, as Robert did in London, to capture a major commission but he was called in to advise as an experienced architect and builder in connection with the early improvements in Edinburgh. In 1752, while he and Robert were working together he had not only drawn up a plan of proposed new approaches to Edinburgh (one wonders how much this resulted from conversations with his younger brothers) but was asked to prepare a plan for a new Exchange off the High Street. His design, although formally accepted in 1753, was taken over and altered by other builders. In 1765, two years after the founding of the North Bridge, he made alterations to the design drawn up by William Mylne and when the structure collapsed he was one of those called in to examine it to try to determine what had been at fault. In 1766, according to a later source, 'Messrs Adams' were asked to comment on James Craig's plan for the New Town and are said to have made alterations to it. Contemporary records certainly identify John as the professional member of a committee to whom Craig's plan was submitted for adjustments before its adoption.[52] In 1766, with the provost, he judged James Craig's proposals for the New Town to be the best of those submitted in the competition. This marginal professional involvement with the transformation of Edinburgh from medieval burgh to modern classical city may have caused even the self-controlled John some disappointment and frustration. In 1760 his failure to gain the commission to build the new Concert Hall, over which the Adams had taken considerable trouble in 1756, resulted in some family recriminations, in which John's brothers suspected he was more offended by the Concert Hall Managers than he cared to admit, while he in turn condemned Robert's revengeful attitude to the successful architect, Robert Mylne, who to the Adams' chagrin had just won the competition to design the new Blackfriars Bridge in London.[53] About this time John was turning over the idea of speculative building near Edinburgh; James commented on this in a letter from Rome in February 1761,

> 'the Estate Peggy mentions as purchas'd near Craigmillar is a sort of foresight
> of John's when Publick works are finish'd, to have ground to build villas on,
> which he imagines will become the taste as soon as the Citizens become rich,
> this was a project talk'd of before I left home'.[54]

A measure of involvement by Robert and James in some of John's commissions was also a feature of the 1760s; building materials and labour were available through John's established trade contacts in order to execute the plans sent from London. Often, however, the plans remained unexecuted, perhaps proving too expensive for the client or beyond the capabilities of a provincial builder, and sometimes they were materially altered. At Moy House, already mentioned, where Colen Williamson took over the work, John Adam was called in and wrote reassuringly to Sir James Grant in the mid-1760s.[55] At Panmure House, Angus, for which Robert prepared an elevation for the west front and plans for stables between 1758 and 1760, the owner, William Maule, Earl of Panmure, asked for a detailed comparison of the building estimate sent from London and that supplied by a Dundee builder; the fact that one of the papers is endorsed with John Adam's name in connection with the plans may be a mere error or an indication that he acted as go-between.[56] One cannot escape the impression that some patrons simply wanted credit for having the good taste to bespeak a design from Robert's prestigious London office, epitomised in the epergne, or ornamental centrepiece for the table, which he designed for the Countess of Findlater in 1768, with which she declared herself delighted. Although no major work was undertaken at Cullen House all three brothers were involved in a succession of minor alterations and improvements over the next 20 years and more. John wrote to the Earl of Findlater and Seafield in 1767 about plans for the approach bridge and a gate for the 'wilderness', and in the same year the Earl asked to see Robert when he came to Scotland in the autumn, although the ceiling designs which he and James prepared that year were apparently not used.[57] In 1768 and 1769 John wrote to the Earl about the interior of the new bedchamber and arranged for the shipment of glass and mirror frames, marble for chimneypieces and iron fittings supplied by the Carron Company. The Earl eventually paid almost £200 for the carving of chimneypieces by top craftsman, Sefferin Nelson, and a painting by Zucchi for a mirror frame, all in connection with designs by Robert and James.[58]

A more important joint project was John's 'contract for the Great Room' at Yester for the 4th Marquess of Tweeddale in 1761.[59] In implementation of this Robert provided the designs for some of the decorative plasterwork and the octagonal coffering of the ceiling. This was the second stage of alterations to James Smith's original house of which the first had been carried out by William Adam. Robert himself was to further transform the great saloon in the late 1780s. In August 1770 Robert and John travelled together to Buchanan House, Stirlingshire, for which the Duke of Montrose had asked Robert for a new plan; the 10 guineas for which Robert gave the Duke's factor a receipt at Buchanan on 29 August may have been for travelling expenses, for he was paid £63.0.0 for the plan a few weeks later.[60] It was 22 years since the Earl of Hopetoun had given the Brothers a testimonial to the Duke as 'Lads' who were well able to carry on their father's work.

Pedestal stove, from an 18th century Carron Company design book; the Company's domestic products began to reflect the Adam revolution in design. *(SRO, Carron Company records: GD58/16/3)*

An association of benefit to both the Scottish and English practices was John's directorship in the Carron Company which he took up in 1763. Not only was he able to supply Adam clients with iron goods, from bath grates for Richard Oswald at Auchincruive to a garden roller for Lord Findlater, but Carron provided cast iron for the external decorative metal work of the Adams' London commissions. The Carron Company on the other hand sought to introduce the fashionable Adam style into their domestic products. In April 1768 they begged John Adam to employ someone to make a variety of designs to help sell the otherwise plain grates in London; 'like a piece of black Cabinet Furniture ... we wish you to put some mouldings or ornaments upon it'. The high Adam manner did not always prove suitable for Carron's robust metalware. In 1772 the design for a vase was returned to the agent in London with the explanation:

> 'it will not cast, nor can we make any alteration without taking away much of the Beauty and destroying the Design. The four ears at the top of the Vaze particularly will not draw out of the sand, as well as the ring that is a little below these ears. You must therefore be so good as to speak to Messrs Adams about it and send a pattern more simple and the figures more strongly impressed'.[61]

In 1764 when Robert's youngest brother William went into partnership with John Wiggins, the clerk in charge of the Carron Company's London warehouse, the firm of Adam and Wiggins became the Company's London agents. At the same time the prestige of the Adams in London and the influence of their second-generation contact with the Ordnance Board were used to maintain the purchase of carronades by the Board.

A BOLD STROKE

The decade which crowned Robert's success in capturing the patronage of fashionable society with the expansion of his English country house practice and the possibility of combining his own flair and John's experience in Scotland to satisfy discerning patrons like the Marquess of Tweeddale or profit-minded businessmen such as the Carron Company, also saw the beginnings of those ambitious ventures and financial problems which were to affect the rest of his working life.

The first stroke of bad luck fell on John with the failure in 1764 of his Edinburgh bankers Adam and Thomas Fairholm, who were also bankers to the Carron Company. Adam Fairholm wrote to his brother Thomas in desperation in March 1764:

> 'I cannot tell how to Account to You and J Adam and the Rest of my Friends for my Strangely mad Ridiculous and Reserved Conduct. I had an immense sum of Profits March last year, but since that every Fund is gone, and I am obliged this day to stop paying £4000 of losses in Holland ... I am demented. I know not what to think or how to Act. My Heart bleeds for my Friends but it bleeds too late. In a fitt of Madness I burned many Accounts and Papers so I cannot make any State of what I have lost, over all profits gained'.[62]

John Adam sat down to work out his own 'State' on paper, down to the skeleton staff which he judged would be necessary to maintain the grounds at Blair House, but eventually decided to put his landed property up for sale. An advertisement duly appeared in the *Caledonian Mercury* of 14 January 1765, offering for sale by public roup 3 houses newly built on his ground in the Cowgate, the lands of Blair, Kinross-shire, and those of North Merchiston, High Riggs with Merchiston House, Ross Park, Sunnyside and Stenhouse Craigs near Edinburgh. No buyers came forward.

Meantime, his brothers, who in the midst of their success had promised that his children should be their children, came forward with a scheme which promised to provide John with financial help and at the same time facilitate the expansion of their own activities in London. In 1764 they set up a firm of property-developers and builders' suppliers to be called William Adam and Company in which all 4 brothers were equal partners, although the Company's finances were for some time kept separate from the architectural practice of Robert and James. Direct participation in the building trade, so as to supply their own undertakings and profit from supplying the operations of others, was a family tradition going back to the industrial enterprises of William Adam. John himself owned timber yards, marble works and brick kilns and leased quarries as far north as Aberdeen from which came paving stones for many London parishes. But the scale of operations now contemplated was new. As far as Robert was concerned, however, the venture into speculative building that followed was almost certainly in order to provide himself with the opportunity which had so far eluded him of making his mark on the townscape of London, a great public statement of his ideas on town-planning and domestic architecture on the grand scale.

At the same time as the partnership sought to provide themselves with the practical means of enhancing their reputation they also took steps to acquire a political base for themselves in influential circles. From 1764 onwards John Adam began to create votes on his property with a view to his or Robert's standing for parliament. In 1768, after a prolonged tussle with other local interests and a law suit, raised by a rival, Robert was elected Member of Parliament for Kinrossshire, the constituency for which Sir William Bruce had been commissioner to the old Scottish Parliament in 1681. So great was Robert's influence with the 'Scotch party' and others in government circles at this time that when he resigned his position as one the Architects to the King's Works in order to stand for parliament, the post was granted to his brother James.

In the year in which Robert became an MP William Adam and Company acquired a prime site in central London, covering just over 3 acres between the Strand and the River Thames, on which to build a prestigious development of first-rate houses. Known as the Durham House estate because in the 16th century it had been occupied by the Bishop of Durham's palace, the property belonged to the trustees of the Duke of St Albans from whom the Adams took a long lease in 1768. William wrote enthusiastically to John on 20 February that year:

> '*Bob and Jamie have secured Durham Yard for the Brotherhood at £1,200 per annum for 99 Years, which you will say is a bold Stroke but it is a noble field and Paine, the architect, etc, etc have since offered more money for it. The Wharf independent of the Ground is worth the rent ... before Bob comes down the survey will be made and the Plans put into some sort of form for your Examination, Approbation and Amendments. It is at present our Hobby Horses*'.[63]

John's fortunes were thus linked with those of his London brothers in their most ambitious family building project ever. The 'noble field' was in fact a sloping site subject to flooding from the river at high tide. With clever planning this liability was turned into a potential asset by building the streets of the development on a series of graded brick arches, higher towards the river, and including in the substructure a line of vaults with access from the adjoining three wharves

on the river front; it was hoped to lease the storage vaults to the Ordnance Board. The most distinguished feature of the Adelphi development (Adelphoi means brothers) was the Royal Terrace, raised high in full view of the Thames river traffic and flanked by the advancing ends of Adam Street, on the east, and Robert Street, on the west, with John Street to the north, parallel to the Terrace; the Adams had written their names on the map of London. Stucco detailing on pilasters, entablatures and string courses accentuated the portions of the brick fronts of the houses which were also adorned with cast-iron balconies, railings and lamps. The interiors were given the full Adam decorative treatment on walls, ceilings, door-cases and chimneypieces. A few of the houses showed more individual planning and external decorative treatment, such as that built between 1772 and 1774 for the Royal Society of Arts to whom it still belongs.

Work proceeded rapidly. Even before the lease from the St Albans Trust was signed (1769) demolition and clearing of the site began. The building activity that followed served as a continual advertisement for the capability of the Adams' architectural practice and building company, employing as it did a large concentration of skilled craftsmen and labourers; there is a story that a piper was hired to keep them in a happy, working mood. But the 'bold stroke' attracted criticism as well as admiration. Robert's avant-garde use of his interior style on the outsides of the houses and the combination of residential and functional

'The Adelphi Terrace', by William Marlow (1740-1813); painted while the buildings were still under construction in the early 1770s. (Reproduced by permission of the National Westminster Bank, PLC)

premises provoked Horace Walpole into describing the buildings as 'Warehouses, laced down the seam, like a soldier's trull in a regimental old coat'.

More serious opposition was marshalled by the City of London and the wharf-men and lightermen of the Thames when it became known that the Company intended to embank part of the river to facilitate access to the vaults. The opposition carried overtones of popular racial resentment:

> *'Four Scotchmen by the name of Adams,*
> *Who keep their coaches and their Madams,*
> *Quoth John in sullen mood, to Thomas,*
> *Have stole the very river from us'.*

Thanks to the support of Robert's friends in parliament a bill authorising the embankment went through in 1771. Although the Company stood to make a fortune from the Adelphi scheme if successfully completed - the ground rents from the houses alone were probably worth over £2,000 a year - the cautious John began to worry about the scale of their advance outlay. In February 1771 he wrote to James, who had asked his opinion on further business ventures:

> *'It is my opinion that we have hitherto attempted too many things and if we had confined ourselves to fewer branches we should have done better'.*[64]

By 1772 the expenses of clearing the site and building had already amounted to over £120,000. In the summer of that year while work was in full swing but the Adephi houses were still not ready for occupation disaster struck a number of London and Edinburgh banks. The Adams had money in several of the affected banking houses and had many bills of exchange in circulation. Unable to pay their own creditors or their workmen, work on the Adelphi was suspended. In June the *Scots Magazine* reported the chaotic state of affairs in London:

> *'Words cannot describe the general consternation of the metropolis on the 22nd. A universal bankruptcy was expected ... The Messrs Adam, of the Adelphi Buildings in the Strand, being unfortunately involved by the failure of some capital houses, upwards of some two thousand valuable artificers and workmen, supported by their undertakings in different parts of the kingdom were thrown out of employment ...'.*

John Adam wrote to a friend before leaving for London to review the family's affairs at first hand:

> *'My Brothers ... have been overwhelm'd in the general Calamity and as they could get no payments have been obliged to stop ... [they] write me that all is confusion and uproar in London ... We are far superior to every debt we owe, So that if times would cooll a little, We have no doubt of putting everything on a very proper footing again ...'.*[65]

Two main solutions to the immediate crisis were hit upon. First, in February 1773, a five-day sale was held by Christie's of many of Robert's and James's collection of paintings and Roman antiquities. John, as a partner in the Company which hoped to benefit from the sale of these assets, wrote in a somewhat more relieved state of mind to his own family in Edinburgh:

'Our sale began today with the pictures ... at very good prices ... on Saturday the drawings will be finished. We have great expectations from these and the statues and other Antiquities, as both these classes are allow'd to be the best of their kinds ever exhibited in England. You cannot conceive the number of people that have come to see them ... We therefore hope for good things'.[66]

There was no shame attached to this kind of sale, in an age of precarious credit and frequent bankruptcies. Rather, there was some pride in demonstrating how 'far superior' were one's assets to the debts exposed by the stroke of ill fortune. In any case, Robert had purchased many of his paintings and sculptures in Italy with investment in mind.

The second expedient, aimed at reducing the Brothers' debts and at the same time ensuring the sale of houses in the Adelphi, was the common 18th century one of a lottery. This was also sanctioned by an act of parliament, Robert making his one and only speech in the House during the debates that surrounded its passing. Horace Walpole was outraged:

'What patronage of the arts in Parliament, to vote the City's land to these brothers, and then sanctify the sale of the houses by a bubble'.

The lottery, on 3 March raised over £200,000, work had resumed on the Adelphi buildings after only a few weeks in 1772 and houses began to sell. The Ordnance Board, however, failed to take up the warehousing. While they escaped actual bankruptcy at this point and were able to survive, the Adelphi crisis had drawn critical public attention to the Adams' activities. Although in a pamphlet explaining the purpose of the lottery the Brothers maintained that they had undertaken the development 'more from an enthusiasm of their own art than from a view of profit' their parliamentary opponents had been convinced that the reverse was the case and from then on critics, whether fellow architects, arbiters of taste or simply tradesmen with a grudge felt free to tilt at the Adam partnership in newspapers and pamphlets. Even while sympathising with them their old friend David Hume doubted the wisdom of such an enormous enterprise:

'Of all the sufferers [in the bank crash] I am the most concerned for the Adams. But their undertakings were so vast that nothing could support them ... To me the scheme of the Adelphi always appeared so imprudent, that my wonder is how they could have gone on so long'.

In the midst of the Adelphi crisis (while they were waiting for the Lottery Act) Robert and James gave themselves a morale boost and their critics a reminder of their many achievements with the publication in 1773 of the first part of *The Works in Architecture of Robert and James Adam*: 'to enable the world to discover where our designs have been imitated with judgement, and where ... servilely copied or misapplied'. With many of the younger generation of architects adopting the Adam style it was time to identify its origin. Almost a decade since the publication of *The Ruins of the Palace of the Emperor Diocletian at Spalatro* (1764), it was time for Robert to demonstrate how he had used his knowledge of the architecture of antiquity. The fact that the text was in English and French showed that the Brothers intended their readership to be international, as indeed did the quality of the production of the plates, some engraved by Bartolozzi and others by Robert's old mentor Piranesi. The first two volumes of *The Works* appeared in parts between 1773 and 1779; a third volume was published posthumously in 1822. There had been many putative Adam publications over the years which did not see print in the family's lifetimes: William's *Vitruvius Scoticus,* John's Garden Designs, James's views of Greece and Robert's proposed revision of Desgodetz. Robert had been thinking of a publication of his own designs from very early in his London practice. On 24 July 1760, in his letter to James about progress on Kedleston he reported that the client himself, Sir Nathaniel Curzon, had spoken

'*about publishing the designs of his House, which I told him I certainly would do soon as all was done & Executed ...*'.

Referring to the drawings then being produced by his Italian recruits he went on,

'*Supposing one could get the Best things they do engraved by degrees, it would produce a Work ... of great value and great Fame, You may perhaps object that this is publishing all your Manner your Ornaments and Studys, That I grant it true, But at the same time I doubt that if you do not publish them yourself Some other will which is worse. Sir Nathaniel's Fronts, may make near 10 plates, including the painted room .... Then there is the Bridge, the Ruins, The Towers, The Pheasant House (a new Contrivance) ... There is Mr Lascelle's plans & fronts, General Blands Room and Green House, and Temple ... then there is my Lord Northumberland, My Lord Coventry, in short many others ... which would make no bad publication already ...*'.[67]

The *Works* certainly flattered the taste of the Adams' major clients as well as advertising the artists' achievements. The Brothers claimed to have brought about 'a kind of revolution in ... this useful and elegant art'. As for the textbook manner of the academic Palladians: 'the massive entablature, the ponderous compartment ceiling, the tabernacle frame [on doors] ... are now universally exploded'. The free, imaginative use of the classical orders was illustrated: 'nothing more sterile and disgustful, than to see forever the dull repetition of Dorick, Ionick and Corinthian entablatures in their usual proportions, reigning round every apartment ...'. 'Movement' in the composition of a building was explained:

'*Movement is meant to express, the rise and fall, the advance and recess, with other diversity of form, in the different parts of a building, so as to add greatly to the picturesque of the composition ... the same effect in architecture, that hill and dale, fore-ground and distance, swelling and sinking have in land-scape'.*

The words echo a passage in one of James's unpublished essays but they also express an essential preoccupation of Robert's - buildings in harmony with their landscape setting.

The *Works* raised a few eyebrows: 'Was there ever such a brace of self-puffing Scotch coxcombs', came from one reader, while Sir William Chambers, from his professional eminence, dismissed the claim of the Adams to have truly interpreted the Antique style. Although it was not in itself a pattern-book the *Works* did help to disseminate the use of the Adam style throughout the building and manufacturing trades.

As has often been stated, there was a certain decline in the Adams' practice in the post-Adelphi years, but it was not immediately apparent. The 1770s (at least the first half of the decade) witnessed some of Robert's finest achievements in London, where the completion of the Adelphi houses and their occupation by many distinguished residents was accompanied by commissions for a number of individual mansions, including those of the Countess of Home in Portman Square, the Earl of Derby in Grosvenor Square, the Duke of Northumberland in the Strand, the Duke of Chandos in Portland Place, and Sir Watkin Williams-Wynn in St James's Square. In their various ways these houses demonstrate Robert's ability as an architect to make an imaginative as well as convenient use of space in narrow city building-plots, as with the staircase at Home House or the internal planning of Derby House where each room led effortlessly to another of different shape. The decoration in this period, almost two-dimensional as in Home House, provides a contrast to the three-dimensional treatment of his early 'Roman' interiors at Syon and Kenwood. The most daring interior of them all was the theatrical drawing room at Northumberland House where he created a glittering setting for the Duke and Duchess's social gatherings with glass walls and pilasters, painted red and green respectively on the back and foiled with shredded gilt copper to give the effect of porphyry, which with the gilded copper decoration were continuously reflected in mirrors.

Similar glass decoration was used in his remodelling of the Theatre Royal, Drury Lane, for his friend and neighbour in the Adelphi David Garrick who had invested like the Duke of Northumberland in the newly-established British Glass-Plate Company at St Helen's, Lancashire. These clients and the architect may have hoped to benefit from a fashion in glass-panelled rooms which, however, did not come about. One critic thought the interior of the new Theatre 'frippery and unmeaning', likely to 'strike the vulgar as very fine', but a first-night audience of about 2000 in 1775 'gave Great applause to the house before the Curtain'.

Even before they had extricated themselves from the financial difficulties of the Adelphi Robert and James were planning further speculative building in the city. Portland Place was intended to be a *Grande Place* of noble houses; an account for designs for a proposed house for the Earl of Findlater estimated a cost of between £16-17,000. Like Mansfield Street, which consisted of less pretentious terrace houses, the Portland Place scheme was hit by the building recession which followed the outbreak of war with the American colonies in 1775. Robert is said to have lost interest in the project on the abandonment of his original concept and to have turned it over to James who designed unified 'palace fronts' for the blocks of terraced houses. In Frederick's Place, Old Jewry, a square containing 8 dwelling houses was built between 1775-6. Apart from Newby Hall, Yorkshire, and Alnwick Castle, Northumberland, where Robert did important work for William Weddell and the Duke and Duchess of Northumberland, respectively, and Saltram, Devonshire, for John Parker, later Lord Boringdon, few major English country house commissions were begun in the 1770s, although there was still some remodelling and interior decoration of parts of existing buildings. It is important, however, that in spite of adverse publicity on the business side of his practice Robert continued to be employed by patrons of the 1760s on the completion of, or alterations and additions to, their houses. A model village was laid out for Sir James Lowther at Lowther in Westmorland, in 1770-5, based on plans of 1766.

Changes were at work, however, which were to influence the course of the second half of Robert Adam's career, in which the difficulties of the early 1770s can be seen as the turning point. A younger generation of architects was coming forward. Some of the best of these by allowing the Adam revolution to influence their style could almost be said to have challenged Robert at his own game; the work of James Wyatt is probably the clearest example of this. Others, such as Henry Holland, favoured a more austere, less decorated and, as they saw it, purer style nearer to that of Adam's rival, Sir William Chambers, which was to gain increasing favour as the century advanced. In 1785, after a visit to Carlton House, then being built by Holland for the Prince of Wales, Horace Walpole exclaimed: 'How sick one shall be, after this chaste palace, of Mr Adam's gingerbread and sippets of embroidery'. This emerging competition and change in taste, the difficult economic circumstances during the American War years, the preoccupation with financial affairs and business deals which must have left Robert and James with less time for strictly architectural work all contributed to bring about a trough in Robert's hitherto ascendant architectural fortunes, a period which lasted from the later 1770s to the mid-1780s.

A change in the balance of Adam family operations also came about in the 1770s with John's withdrawal from architectural practice. Tragically, his financial losses in the combined Fairholm and Adelphi disasters put an end to his plans to transform his house at the Blair, the improvement of which had begun with his own court of offices in 1760 and ended with Robert's grand design for the enlargement of the house itself, drawn in the midst of the troubles of 1772. The financial crisis apart, it might have been difficult for John to maintain a busy practice alone in the long run; in 1760 he had claimed that he was turning away work.[68] In any case, he was by the 1770s deriving a comfortable return from his shares in the Carron Iron Company and continued to do so. John's retirement from practice held out the possibility of an expansion of Robert's and James's interests in Scotland to fill the gap. From about 1772, probably because their major public commission for the Register House was begun that year with the acceptance of the plans, they set up an office in Edinburgh, under the charge of a clerk of works but with John available as consultant when required.

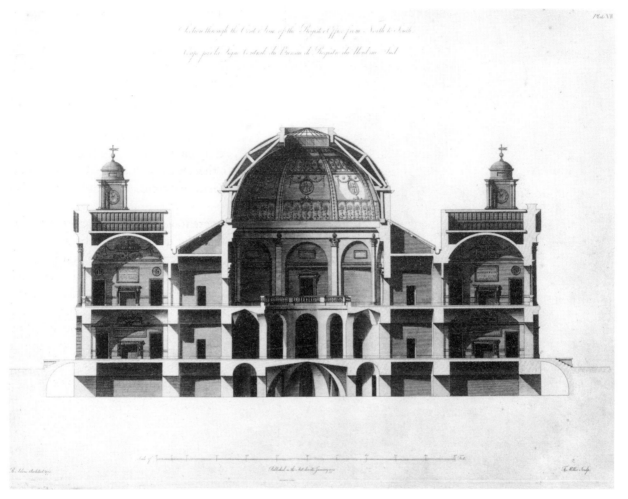

The General Register House, Edinburgh: section through the building from North to South; Robert Adam, 1771. *(The Works in Architecture of Robert and James Adam; plate in Register House Plans, 6082)*

NOT *at* COURT

Successful though he was in the fashionable metropolis, where his activities were the subject of public comment, personal references to Robert Adam and his family in the letters and diaries of the period are few and almost all associated with his work. The famous description by his client Mrs Montagu of his arrival at her house in the summer of 1779 has preserved a glimpse of him in the days when, dapper, self-confident and as quick off the mark as ever his father had been, he could still make a very personal contribution to the image of his profession - except that on this occasion he was late:

> 'He came at the head of a regiment of artificers an hour after the time he had promised: the bricklayer talked an hour about the alterations to be made in a wall, the stonemason was as eloquent about the coping ..., the carpenter thought the internal fitting up of the house not less important, then came the painter who is painting my ceilings in various colours according to the present fashion. The morning and my spirits were quite exhausted before these important persons had the goodness to release me'.

Architects like Paine and Brettingham whom he supplanted at several commissions do not seem to have borne him a grudge; Paine had some interest in part of the Durham Yard development site and suffered accordingly. James 'Athenian' Stuart and Robert 'Blackfriars' Mylne, although the Adams privately disparaged some of their works, remained on outwardly friendly terms with them. Also on good terms was the young John Nash to whom the Adams apparently loaned money for his own speculative ventures, to his financial embarrassment.[69] The personal friendship, even rapport, which Robert maintained with many clients over the years gave him a useful lever in getting things to happen from time to time; in a letter to his nephew William, for whose re-election to parliament he was canvassing support, he could speak of having written 'a very warm letter last night to Lord Mansfield which brought him here this morning ... I have a notion the body will do more than he says'.[70] Yet on another occasion, in 1781, he had to apologise to Lord Buchan for being unable to pull strings in royal circles;

'My own situation at court, or rather my own situation not at court, prevents me from having it in my power to do what would have been very pleasing to me on this occasion, and what is worse, my having no correspondence with Sir William Chambers puts it out of my power to use that vehicle of intelligence, nor have I yet been able to find out any other person who could apply, or whose application would carry weight along with it'.[71]

Chambers, scholarly and authoritative, the establishment professional *par excellence*, deplored Robert Adam's almost lighthearted treatment of their art, as he saw it. The allegation that he prevented Robert's election to the Royal Academy and receipt of a knighthood cannot be proved but may be true, although the Adams were on friendly terms with the Academy's President, Sir Joshua Reynolds.

Closest personal friends came mainly from the Scots community in London and those Scots who came up to the city from time to time: John Home for whose house of Kilduff, East Lothian, Robert 'schemed two wings' in 1770 'to give him the conveniencys necessary for a married man'; General Hugh Debbieg whom he had first met in the 1750s when Debbieg was employed with Paul Sandby on the military survey of Scotland; Allan Ramsay, his old Roman 'crony' whom he caught up with again after the latter's return to Britain in 1777, 'who is in wonderful good spirits and is grown fatter since he came to England though not able to bustle for want of his limbs'; and Alexander Carlyle who, when in London, 'resorted often to supper at Robert Adam's, whose sisters were very agreeable, and where we had the latest news from the House of Commons of which he was a Member, and which he told us in the most agreeable manner and with very lively comments'.

Frances (Fanny) D'Arblay (née Burney, 1752-1849), writer, one of the few social commentators who record meeting Robert Adam; portrait by E F Burney. *(National Portrait Gallery, London)*

The most vivid recollection of Robert's sociable nature has been left by the young Fanny Burney who met him with others of 'the Scotch party' at the house of General and Mrs Debbieg in March 1770:

'... Mr Adams, very sensible, very polite and very agreeable - the most so, Mr Debbieg excepted, of the whole party, Mr Adams his younger brother, a well-behaved good sort of young man ... We began dancing about 9 o'clock ... Then we left off for supper. During the time of rest I was happier than in dancing, for I was more pleased with the conversations I then had with Mr Dundas, Mr Adams and others, than with my partners ... Mr Dundas the elder and Mr Adams are quite high conversers ...

When supper was over, all who had voices worth hearing were made to sing - none shone more than Mr Adams; though in truth he has little or no voice, ... yet he sung with so much taste and Feeling, that few very fine voices could give equal pleasure; I cannot but much regret the probability there is of my never seeing him again ...'.[72]

Some 20 years later Peggy Adam was to remember 'a dancing that we had many a long year since at Mrs Debbieg's and Mrs Pringle's and our house, but if I remember we had no musick but Archy Robertson's flute and Sir Archibald Campbell's fiddle ...'.

The problem of how to dispose the family between Edinburgh and London, which had so exercised Robert in Italy, was solved, sadly, by the death of Mrs Adam from a heart attack in 1761 shortly after she had returned home from a visit to Robert in his new London home. James, then in Italy alone, was particularly devastated by the news. Peggy then broke up the family home and joined her brothers and sisters, Jenny and Betty, in London; she was to outlive them all except William. With her she must have taken the bundles of Robert's letters from Italy which were to return to Scotland with her niece Susan Clerk early in the next century. Throughout the triumphs and trials of the next decade and a half family solidarity was maintained. Scottish relatives, like those of other Scots families before and since, spent holidays with their relatives in London, including their brother-in-law 'Jock' Clerk of Eldin whom Robert took to see work in progress on some of his commissions.

John Adam's sons, 'frank, open and pleasant' William, as Robert described him, and his younger, more modest brother, John, who died while still a schoolboy, were both a source of family pride. In July 1769 Robert threw his weight against the opinion of Dr William Robertson and others who had been trying to persuade John Adam to take his younger son away from Eton where he was making good progress and put him to the College at Edinburgh.[73] 'If he is to be a John Bull', Robert argued, he should continue his education in the south. 'When a man is to push through life for himself, the sooner he feels no prop the better', he wrote, recalling how 'when your Willie came to London [from Oxford] Jock and he read and Construed Horace and other Authors together ... Jamie, Uncle Willie and I were hearers ...'. Only four months later John, writing to his factor, intimated the death of his younger son.

'Mrs Adam you may believe is in the utmost affliction, as we are all here [Edinburgh]; and what adds greatly to it is that my Brothers and Sisters in London have suffered extremely both from their anxiety of Mind and fatigue of body, for some one or other of them never left him night nor day ... It is the severest blow I have ever experienced'.[74]

It had been envisaged that the next generation of the family would not simply migrate to the south but begin their careers there. William was to have a distinguished career as a barrister and Member of Parliament. There are occasional glimpses of the reflected glory which his family derived from his progress as a young parliamentarian. In October 1775, by which time Robert's household was installed in Number 4 Royal Terrace, The Adelphi, his brother William wrote glowingly to John:

'I am happy to confirm to you from every quarter the highest approbation of Willie's speech [in the Commons] on Friday last. Adam Smith who was there supped with us last night. He says ... that Lord North's was the best Speech ... and that Willie's was the next ... Bob dined on Sunday with Mr Rigby, where was Lord Ossery, Mr Fitzpatrick, Mr Garrick ... who all agreed that Willie's was a very extraordinary Speech ...'.[75]

In 1771, the year in which the Adelphi embankment got the go-ahead and before the bank crisis had cast a shadow over his 'bold stroke' in the centre of London, Robert paid for an elegant addition to the recently- repaired County Court House at Kinross at the heart of his Scottish parliamentary constituency.

Classical and vernacular; the southern end of the County Court House, Kinross (left), embellished by Robert Adam as MP for the shire in 1771. *(Royal Commission on the Ancient and Historical Monuments of Scotland)*

This consisted of a bowed projection at the southern end of the building where, between pilasters and above the centre window of the first floor, an inscription was placed:

'This County House was
Repaired by the Crown
A.D.1771
ROBERT ADAM KNIGHT
of this shire decorated
this front at his own
Expense'.

This local advertisement for the MP's professional skill stopped John Adam's son William in this tracks when he saw it. His comments caused his father to reply,

'I am sorry if either the Inscription looks Ostentatious or the Execution looks mean ... there are pilasters, with an Entablature over them And there are Niches and pannels, all which would have been plain, if your Uncle had not chose to be at the expense of them'.[76]

Young William Adam, making his name in London, may have found the squibs recently thrown at Adam pretensions there something of an embarrassment. But, even if the decoration of the Court House may have raised a smile, the Adams were generally treated with respect in Scotland, where they belonged to the society that produced their clients and their reputation was built on their father's achievements, John's experience and the success of Robert and James in London which was regarded at home with pride. For every obstructionist during the execution of Robert's later commissions in Scotland there were usually several champions, as there were, for example, during the building of the College of Edinburgh.

Robert's personal Scottish commissions began to build up from the mid-1770s onwards, as those of John decreased, the numbers accelerating from the late 1780s onwards after a particularly painful decline in creative output in the first half of that decade. In contrast to the general pattern of his earlier career they were often for entire buildings, including some important public works. He was aware by the time the emphasis of his practice swung northwards of the various proposals for the further development of Edinburgh, in both the area where he had grown up on the edge of the Old Town and in the New Town itself, and must have hoped to make his mark on the city to whose dramatic landscape setting he was particularly sensitive. He was 47 by the time the Adelphi was completed. Before his later Scottish work had been taken seriously by historians it was said that if Robert had died at that age he would still have been one of the greatest architects of the 18th century, which is true. Nevertheless, we would not now speak of his remaining 17 years as 'the period of unfulfilment', as one historian did in 1947. In fact, what awaited him in Scotland, the 'narrow place' which he had left in the 1750s, might almost be called a second career.

lthough at no time during the accomplishment of their 'Revolution' in the south had Robert and James been cut off from Scotland, it is more likely, given the extent of Robert's English country house practice and London work, that Scottish patrons of the 1760s sought him out than that he cultivated commissions north of the Border. In any case, a number of these clients had close links with the south, for example, Lord Findlater and Richard Oswald of Auchincruive. From the mid-1770s onwards, however, it is possible to think of Robert's Scottish practice as something more substantial and continuous. To take his designs for classical houses alone, it has been estimated that one-third of all these were for Scottish clients, 10 out of 50 during the 1760s and 1770s but 26 Scottish as against 10 English houses after 1780. When to the classical houses are added those in what Robert and James called their 'castle style', most of which were for Scottish clients from the 1770s onwards, the geographical swing in the Adams' later practice is seen to be dramatic. As already mentioned, an office was set up in Edinburgh from which business was dispatched and where drawings were sometimes prepared. Letters and business papers have preserved many details of how the architects kept in touch with their Scottish clients, officials and tradesmen.

Although a clerk of works was usually appointed for major commissions Robert and James were able to maintain overall control of their most important works. They charged 50 guineas for travelling and subsistence for each journey from London to inspect those works of which they were appointed surveyors (in addition to architects) even when, as at the Register House in Edinburgh, a full-time clerk of works had been appointed. Robert usually lived on his visits to Edinburgh with one or other of his married sisters and her husband, Dr and Mrs Drysdale in Shakespeare Square, John and Susannah Clerk in Princes Street and, latterly, with the widowed Mary Drysdale in Nicolson Street, although in 1786 he boarded at Dunn's Hotel. Travel was by hired post-chaise, which enabled him to make his own time and was convenient for transporting portfolios of drawings, including the full-scale drawings for workmen, which Robert sometimes carried with him. Drawings were required in Edinburgh whether the architect contemplated a journey or not and he often sent them in boxes on the mail coach after it began running between London and Edinburgh in 1786. This involved risk of losing them as well as the advantage of a new 3-day delivery time. John Paterson, clerk of works at the College of Edinburgh, assured him on 14 March 1790:

'I sent yesterday per the Mail Coach the plans of the Bridewell [to be built on Calton Hill] and the original papers of Dr Munro and Black's classes [at the College] which you thought you had lost, however the Estimate must be lost or stolen together with your own Observations ... as they positively were packed up with your other papers'.[77]

Robert had an arrangement of charging for plans alone without his further involvement in the work. Some clients, to save expense, opted simply to purchase plans from the famous designer and hand them over to a local architect to oversee execution or to a competent builder to implement them directly in consultation with themselves. In some cases this resulted in modifications or alterations to the original design, or to its abandonment as too costly or beyond the capabilities of the local tradesmen. There was a scale of charges for the plans. In later years at least, according to his sister Mrs Drysdale,

'Robie's rule here [Edinburgh] was that if a house was not to cost five hundred Pound he charged twenty Pound for the Plan, if it came above a thousand then he charged one per cent ... I know it was his way to charge the Plans that was not taken as well as those that were'.[78]

In the case of commissions which were built over several years additional drawings would be made and charged for from time to time. On the other hand the architect might waive charges if he so wished. In 1791 he gave William Nisbet of Dirleton a discount of 10 guineas on the return of drawings for the interior of Archerfield House, East Lothian, which had not been used; this, one assumes, had not been due to the client's having changed his mind.[79]

Buildings in the landscape; in this undated ink and water-colour drawing by Robert Adam the landscape dominates the picture, the castle being almost part of the sky-line. *(The Trustees of the National Galleries of Scotland)*

At his discretion he might credit the cost of the plans towards his surveyor's fee, if appointed to oversee the work personally. The fee was first set at $2\frac{1}{2}$ per cent but later rose to 5 per cent of the cost of building. The latter was estimated by a 'measurer' on the quantities and prices of materials required to erect and finish the house according to the plans. Alexander Ponton, the Edinburgh measurer, costed Robert Adam's late Scottish commissions and on one occasion accompanied him to Dunbar while the Earl of Lauderdale's house there was being built. The architect expected to be paid for substantial advice which in his view amounted to surveying, and to avoid doubt in this matter his appointment as surveyor was usually agreed on formally with the client. It was a misunderstanding in this respect that led to a breakdown in relations with the client of Airthrey Castle, Stirlingshire, Captain Robert Haldane, whom he claimed had employed him both as architect and surveyor and then abandoned him for the services of the Russells, the builders of another late commission, Seton Castle. A similar situation with the nephew of his lifelong friend John Home, Captain Home of Ninewells, was avoided when Robert decided

> '*to make no demand on Captain Home for anything I have done for him as Surveyor ... Having such intimacy for many years with his uncle, I should hate to have the smallest difference with any of his nephews*'.

Nevertheless, he explained the reason for his termination of the commission to the client's brother, John Home, WS:

> '*When I am employed to make designs only I am paid for my plan and have done with the business, such was the case when your Brother received his Plans and paid me the £21. But the case was totally changed when he desired other alterations on the Plan and calculating of timbers and ... I had examined his quarry rock and at his desire I looked out for a quarrier and recommended one. In short I was proceeding in every step as a surveyor to his Building and I never doubted that we all understood it so. But to wish to be employed when not agreeable to the employer would be the hight of folly in me ... But it has always been and always will be a maxim of mine that when confidence ceases the business ought to end as quick as possible – and still better if it is never begun*'.[80]

The difficulties that arose out of the tradesmen's opposition to Robert's claim as surveyor to fix the prices for workmanship at the College have been fully chronicled. On 15 February 1791 John Clerk of Eldin reported to the family in London on the triumph of the Adam lobby at a Trustees' meeting after which he was invited by Robert's champion, the advocate Henry Erskine, 'to drink a bottle of his best claret to the health of Bob Adam and the College'. The Earl of Hopetoun, who arrived late at the meeting, declared that he would withhold his subscription to the College should opposition to Robert continue, while 'Mr Solicitor Blair nodded to everything Harry Erskine said'.[81] The conduct of business on this scale had its political as well as practical problems.

Clients naturally wished the final appearance of their houses to reflect their own taste and might voice their preferences from time to time during the progress of the work. When this was done in full consultation with the architect friction was avoided. A letter from Robert to his client at Mellerstain, George Baillie of Jerviswood, in the spring of 1778 highlights both this diplomatic aspect and various practical considerations.

'I see no objection to your putting ornaments in these spaces though the ceiling should remain plain, as they belong to the upright walls of the room and have no connection with the ceiling. I shall return you the drawing of the gallery ornament so soon as I have your answer, as I shall immediately make account and send you the parts of the ornaments at large for decorating the execution. Have you got another plaisterer since you parted with Powell? I am sorry he behaved so ungratefully.

I shall do my best to please you in the drawings you desire for your ceilings ... They shall be plain and elegant and not expensive ...'.[82]

Sophisticated details of interior decoration were sometimes sent from London. These mostly came by sea, like the bas-reliefs for the Dome ceiling of the Register House, but some came by road, such as the plaster figures for Archerfield which travelled on the 'London Waggon'. Wooden moulds for plasterwork were sent on the Mail Coach (one can understand why there were complaints about the overloading of these vehicles). Robert wrote to his Edinburgh clerk of works, John Paterson,

'The mouldings for Seton Castle I had begun sometime ago ... and will send them by Mail Coach some day next week, and also the mouldings for Lord Lauderdale's house at Dunbar except the frizes which I think had better be modelled here [London] and sent down by Sea ...'.

Much depended on having a competent clerk of works at the Scottish end. James Salisbury, an Englishman, was recommended to the Trustees of the Register House by Robert and James as someone 'in whose honesty, diligence, sobriety and capacity [they] had already had great experience'. Salisbury, a master-carpenter, was also given the carpentry contract for the building; it is sad that the handsome mahogany model of the Register House which he made is now missing. With a salary of £100 a year, apart from his carpentry contract, he did well enough out of the project to be able to buy property in the proposed Leith Street development.

Hugh Cairncross, who practised as an architect after Robert Adam's death, was clerk of works at Culzean and Dalquharran Castles in Ayrshire and from December 1791, at the College of Edinburgh. The tradesmen's accounts which survive and his own account book illustrate his responsibilities at Culzean during the later phase of building.[83] William Cairncross, presumably a relative, who was carpenter at Culzean, travelled to London to consult the architect in the Spring of 1778 and on his return to Scotland called at Mellerstain at request of Robert Adam to hand in finished ceiling designs before going on to Ayrshire.[84]

John Paterson was clerk of works at some of Robert's most important late commissions including the College, Seton Castle and the Earl of Lauderdale's house at Dunbar, until he had a disagreement with the Adams and left their service at the end of 1791 while Robert was himself in Scotland. Yet, the latter owed much to Paterson's positive approach to his role; it was his encounter with the Stirling brothers that gained his master his important Glasgow commissions and a breakthrough in his practice in the west of Scotland, while his initiative persuaded the Provost and magistrates of Edinburgh to transfer the commission for what became Charlotte Square from James Nisbet to Robert Adam. As an architect in his own right in later years Paterson showed that he had absorbed the main principles of the Adam style in 'castle-style' houses and room-planning. In 1790 he persuaded Lord Lauderdale to use the lighter Craigleith rather than red East Lothian stone for his house, as he explained to Robert Adam:

> '[I] advised him to fix on some other Stone of a white collour that would give his House a much lighter appearance. The sun shining on the white stone would express the shade and consequently the movement of your Design ... and added I was certain you would give his Lordship the same advice'.

Paterson wrote assiduously to his master about every stage of the various works, especially the College where on 19 March 1791 he reported joyfully,

> 'I am so very throng about erecting our large Collumns at the entry of the College and has the pleasure of informing you that I have got one of them erected this day at twelve o'cloack without the Smallest Accident takeing place and very much to the Satisfaction of every person heare and is Certain it will be much more so to You who was the projector of so Noble an undertaking'.

The six great 22 feet-high monolithic columns form a splendid piece of Adamesque flamboyance, giving the College entrance the character of a triumphal arch.

> 'It gives me much pleasure', Robert replied, 'to hear that the Columns are rising on the East Front ... I hope to see something handsome when I get down'.

It was in Scotland that Robert fully developed his 'castle-style' which he had been experimenting with since the mid-1760s. The tendency of earlier historians to underestimate his later Scottish work led to his being traditionally regarded as an interior designer whose work links more naturally with the decorative arts, than as a serious architect in the robust, three-dimensional world of building. In 1922 his biographer A T Bolton, who was also custodian of the magnificent collection of drawings from the Adam office, said of his castles that they were 'essentially false and led to nothing', while those who disliked the Scots baronial style that came later blamed him for starting it. Only after studying the Adam castles objectively in their own right can a modern historian rank them 'amongst the most original creations of 18th-century European architecture'.[85]

There is a debate among historians as to where Robert got his inspiration for his castle-style houses but most agree that considering the kind of artist he was, who gleaned from his experience many ideas which he blended into a very individual style, there are likely to have been different sources of inspiration. These include the castles of the Italian landscape, ancient or Renaissance, which he drew at first-hand. Some historians see the castles partly as Robert's contribution to the Gothic style, bearing in mind his early interest in Gothic buildings and the impression made on him and his brothers by Inveraray in the 1750s. He could design in the Gothic manner when requested, as in the interiors of Alnwick Castle, for the Duke and Duchess of Northumberland, or the unexpected Gothic ceiling in a corridor at Mellerstain, but there are no pointed windows like those of Inveraray in any of his castles, and those medieval features which he continued to use were associated with defence, such as arrow-slits in the towers and battlements at the wallheads. We know that he had a continuing interest in fortifications from his boyhood when, according to John Clerk, he often built them, complete with cannon. His first personal responsibilities were associated with the building of a real Fort, at Ardersier, while for much as his career he had professional contact with the work of the Ordnance Board.

The Scottish influence is an obvious one in the castle-style. Great round defensive towers, which could be either Italian or Scottish, feature in most of the romantic landscapes which he painted during those years when the castles were being developed, but although some of these were inspired by Italy the mood of the landscapes often appears Scottish, where these buildings seem particularly at home. While it is likely that Robert's overriding interest in them was aesthetic, that of his Scottish clients may have been quite different; to them castles were associated not only with defence but with ancient lineage and established terri-

Buildings in the landscape: Robert Adam's own ink and watercolour drawing of Oxenfoord Castle, Midlothian, which he designed for his friend Sir John Dalrymple; undated. *(Reproduced by permission of Keith Adam of Blair Adam)*

torial possession. Clients like George Baillie at Mellerstain, William Mure at Caldwell and the Earl of Cassillis at Culzean were all building modern houses in parts of the country where their families had long been powerful. Even Sir John Dalrymple, who shared the architect's love of landscape, wrote to a friend in 1784 about his own new house, Oxenfoord Castle, Midlothian.

'I am always happy to hear from you but would be happier to see you in this country where I have repaired a noble old castle and by the help of Bob Adams have really made it much older than it was, ... it would suit you, who are an Antiquary, perfectly'.

The first of Robert Adam's Scottish castle-style houses of the 1770s, like the still earlier examples of the 1760s in Scotland and England, were externally plain to the point of being severe yet they gradually show more of the dramatic features that were to characterise the later castles. Most severe of them all, and the first to be started, is Mellerstain, Berwickshire (1770-8), where Robert designed the central block between two wings begun by his father in 1725. The external appearance of the house is almost fort-like, with the slightly advancing centre and end portions of the main and garden fronts and the long battlemented wall-heads on the skyline providing the only relief. The layout of the main rooms follows the linear character of the exterior; there are no planning surprises inside. It is sometimes remarked that this planning and the severe exterior are uncharacteristic of Robert Adam. They may reflect the taste of the client George Baillie who, as we saw, sent the architect some general drawings of what he required, expecting an 'elegant and not expensive' design in return. The decoration of the interiors, however, especially the ceilings, is as sophisticated as that of any classical Adam house. The library, which has been described as having 'the effect of perfection', can be compared in quality with that at Osterley. The gallery at the top of the house, on the other hand, with its vaulted ceiling, is a feature found in many Scottish castles and may be seen at Craigievar.

An early Scottish castle by Robert Adam: Wedderburn, Berwickshire, 1771-5. *(Royal Commission on the Ancient and Historical Monuments of Scotland. Photograph, Professor Alistair Rowan)*

Wedderburn, Berwickshire, built (1771-8) for Patrick Home of Billy from a branch of the great Home family who had dominated the East March for centuries, was given a more castle-like character, having a central bow on the south front and octagonal-shaped corner towers which rose higher than the main block. Yet the basement was made of 'rusticated' blocks as was usual in Palladian houses to give them a look of stability, and 'string courses' ran across the facade separating the storeys. It was still a classical house given the castle treatment.

William Mure of Caldwell, baron of the Scottish Exchequer, former MP for Renfrewshire and manager of the Earl of Bute's Scottish estates, was influential in political circles and on a sufficiently personal footing with all the Adam brothers for Robert to ask his advice on the valuation of the Blair estate in 1772 when John contemplated raising a loan on his property. In earlier times the Mures had been influential in Ayrshire from Cunningham in the north to Carrick in the south. Their castles included Caldwell near Beith, on the border of Ayrshire and Renfrewshire, which William Mure planned to replace with his new house, and Rowallan from which had come the consort of King Robert II (1371-90). The first scheme for the new house was classical but the client preferred the castle-

The Adam 'revolution' expressed in a Scottish country house: the Library at Mellerstain House, Berwickshire. *(Royal Commission on the Ancient and Historical Monuments of Scotland)*

style. Although rectangular with shallow projections, like Mellerstain and some even earlier English castle-style houses by Robert, Caldwell carries some undoubted features of a fortified building, notably the machicolation which runs round under the battlements and the round bartizans at the corners of the wall-head, both of which became regular features of the later fully-developed Adam castles.

The first building-phase of Culzean castle was the highlight of Robert's work for private Scottish clients in the decade of the 1770s, although to appreciate his achievement to the full the entire development of the design from 1772 until his death 20 years later has to be taken into account. The forebears of David 10th Earl of Cassillis, advocate, Member of Parliament for Ayrshire in the same session as Robert Adam sat for Kinross-shire, soldier and, like his architect, earlier Grand Tourist in Italy, were the most powerful family in the sheriffdom in feudal times;

> *'Twixt Wigtoune and the town of Aire*
> *And Laigh down by the Cruives of Cree,*
> *You shall not get a lodging there,*
> *Except you court wi' Kennedy'.*

Castellated mansion for a client of ancient lineage: Caldwell House, Ayrshire, designed for William Mure, 1773-4. *(SRO, Register House Plans, 2549)*

After designing a more modest building for the 9th Earl, who died towards the end of 1775 before work could begin, Robert and James embarked two years later on the grand transformation of the site of the ancient keep of the Kennedys.

The first phase of building was the construction of a suite of rooms occupying the space of the old tower and its immediate vicinity; in the early 1780s the kitchen wing, which included other functional premises such as the brewhouse, cold bath and dressing room, was added; from 1785 the most dramatic and boldly-modelled north elevation was built on the edge of the cliffs looking sea-wards, with the great round tower which contains the magnificent saloon. The *tour de force* was the construction of the oval staircase at the heart of the space formerly occupied by the old keep, to do which work already completed had to be taken out. Columns surround the staircase, the capitals arranged by Robert not in academic sequence but as Doric, Corinthian (in the central position where they are most appreciated as one climbs the stair) and Ionic. Building accounts record the work not only of international artists such as Van Gelder who carved chimney pieces but of local craftsmen such as John McClure of Ayr who was responsible for the plaster work of ceilings and the galleries on the staircase.

The concurrence of circumstances, the opportunity to develop his design over the years, the dramatic natural setting and a sympathetic – and wealthy – patron must have made Culzean one of Robert's most satisfying commissions. His brother-in-law, John Clerk of Eldin, who travelled with him to inspect the work at the castle in the autumn of 1788 over countryside in which they had sketched together, called it

> '*the whimsical but magnificent Castle of Colane ... on which the Earl ... encouraged him to indulge to the utmost his romantic genius*'.

The dramatic approach to the Castle through the ancient-seeming archway and across a ravine might have been taken from one of his own picturesque landscapes and seems to capture the romantic mood in which he conceived the castle's design, evolutionary though this was.

Another source of satisfaction in the early 1770s was the opportunity to design a monumental public building of national importance on a site in the New Town of Edinburgh, the General Register House. The need for 'a proper repository'

Auchincruive teahouse, Ayrshire, 1778. The Georgian fashion for a garden-building in which to take tea is rendered into a perfect little castellated building by Robert Adam – a tower on rising ground, complete with machicolation and battlements. *(Royal Commission on the Ancient and Historical Monuments of Scotland)*

for the national records was keenly felt by mid-18th century and the various schemes put forward must have been known to the Adams for some time. One suggestion had been to house the records in rooms in the new Exchange designed by John Adam in 1753 as part of the civic improvements in Edinburgh. Credit for a positive scheme to raise money for a purpose-built repository goes to the Earl of Morton, Clerk Register from 1760 to 1768, whose personal inspection of the appalling storage conditions in the Laigh Parliament House and elsewhere brought the matter to a head. It was to the Adams' friend and future client,

Patron who allowed Robert Adam to indulge 'his romantic imagination' at Culzean: David Kennedy, 10th Earl of Cassillis. Painted by Batoni in Rome in 1764. *(The National Trust for Scotland)*

Tour de force at Culzean; the magnificent oval staircase created on the site of the medieval keep at the heart of the 18th century castle. *(The National Trust for Scotland)*

William Mure of Caldwell, that Morton wrote in 1763 about the difficulty of raising funds for the project. In 1765 a crown grant of £12,000 was made from the funds of the Forfeited Estates Commissioners and a plan of the proposed building was devised by the Clerk Register himself and drawn by an architect two years later.

Morton died in 1768 with his ambition unrealised. His successor, Lord Frederick Campbell, a son of the 4th Duke of Argyll, was a friend of Robert and James Adam who were then working on alterations to his house at Ardincaple, Dunbartonshire, and were soon to do the same at his English home of Combe Bank in Kent. The new Clerk Register lost no time in pushing the commission firmly in the direction of the Adams. In November 1770 Robert was in Edinburgh 'about Register Office business',[86] the plans, elevations and section of the new building as published in *The Works in Architecture* are dated 1771 and on the 30 July 1772, when the Trustees recorded that the Clerk Register had 'employed Messrs Robert and James Adam, Architects, to draw a Plan of a proper Repository for the Records of Scotland', Lord Frederick signed the south elevation of the building in token of their acceptance.[87] The Trustees, apart from the Clerk Register, consisted of Robert Dundas of Arniston (Lord President of the Court

'A Proper Repository': the General Register House soon after it had begun to function as the earliest purpose-designed record repository in the British Isles. The building stands, in this 1805 drawing, in elegant contrast to the pro-saic housing in early Princes Street. *(Drawn by A Carse, engraved by R Scott)*

of Session), Thomas Miller of Glenlee (Lord Advocate), Sir Gilbert Elliot, Robert Adam's old friend who had helped to win him his very first public commission in London, the Admiralty screen, and Robert Orde, for whom Robert had recently designed a handsome town house in Queen Street on the skirts of the New Town (Chief Baron of the Scottish Exchequer).

The foundation stone of the Register House was laid on 27 June 1774. James Boswell, who was present was scathing about the lack of ceremony and poked fun at the Clerk Register, 'Lord Freddie with a foolish face' who 'tripped about delicately'.

'I was very angry that there was no procession, no shew or solemnity of any kind upon such an occasion. There was a fine sight both of well-drest people and mob; so that there was spirit enough in the country to relish a Shew; and such things do good. It should have been laid either privately in the morning; or with some dignity. But cards were sent to all the Judges, as private men, and they accordingly dropped in, one by one, without their gowns, and several of them with Bob wigs. The Lord Provost too was there as a private man. To appear so soon at noon before a Crowd of spectators was very poor.

The occasion, nevertheless, was enlivened with salutes of gunfire and refreshments were provided by a Captain Ferguson of the Navy who was thanked for 'so agreeably entertaining the company who attended on an occasion of so very great importance to the country in general'. To be associated in his profession with public authority in this way must have given Robert considerable satisfaction at this juncture in his career, when he had just escaped the worst consequences of an over-ambitious private venture in London. Ironically, as has been pointed out, Sir William Chambers was to even the odds two years later with the appearance in London of Somerset House, a little further downriver from the Adelphi.[88] But meantime Robert celebrated with Edinburgh friends. Two days after the founding of the Register House, at a dinner party given by Baron Mure of Caldwell, Boswell met 'Bob Adams, the Architect, who was lively enough, though vain, for which I forgave him' and two days later still he and Robert and another of the latter's Edinburgh clients, the sociable lawyer Andrew Crosbie, were among those who were 'sufficiently jovial' at Lord Monboddo's, after which 'to go home to business seemed dull'.

The Register House stands at the meeting place of Old and New Edinburgh visually terminating what was the first major route between them. The elevations are dressed in restrained Palladian good taste. The ground plan is the simple and eminently convenient one of a domed central hall within a rectangular block of working offices. This was Robert's interpretation of a design of Antiquity, such as that of the Pantheon, which had so impressed him in Rome. A great central dome within a square, had been part of his plan for Syon but was not executed. The entire Register House, except for the inner structure of the dome ceiling and the floor of the Clerk Register's Room above the entrance hall is built of stone (from the local Craigleith and Ravelston quarries) to reduce the risk of fire. The loadbearing potential of the stone floors lessens the problem of storing heavy record volumes. The 'crossing-point' provided by the central saloon facilitates the movement of people and records around the building.

Apart from the 8 bas-reliefs, on classical themes, which were shipped from London, the plasterwork of the dome ceiling (begun in 1785) was carried out by Thomas Clayton, younger.[89] The decoration closely follows that shown on the section through the building from north to south, illustrated in *The Works in Architecture*, except for the alteration of the rib decoration from bell-flowers to double guilloche scrolls, the shortening of the bottom band of decoration and a reduction in the size of the bas-reliefs. The thistles and roses in the lower frieze strike a British note. The proposed stone balustrade in the dome gallery was altered during construction to the existing cast-iron railing with wooden handrail.

There were two phases of building, 1774-78 and 1785 until the late 1820s; the Office was functioning in a partially-constructed building by about 1788. The Minutes of the Trustees, with many accounts, letters and other papers, demonstrate the ability of Robert and James to conduct the undertaking from London, with James Salisbury on the site and John Adam available as consultant if need be.[90] At the same time Robert was often contacted about practical matters, paid some tradesmen's bills and countersigned others and when he did pay a surveyor's visit made a thorough inspection of the work. He insisted on a high standard of workmanship at all times and sent some of the materials from London, such as the famous Liardet stucco for the external decorative details including the royal coat-of-arms on the pediment. He recommended English bricklayers for the first phase of the building, finding the Scots deficient in that branch of the work, and persuaded the Trustees to choose lead rather than slates for the dome and pediment roofs as being 'more beautiful' if a little more expensive.

Design for a chimneypiece for the second drawing room for Baron Robert Orde's house in Queen Street, Edinburgh, 1771. Robert Adam is known to have produced over 500 designs for chimneypieces which, to many people, have become the symbolic feature of his style. *(Royal Commission on the Ancient and Historical Monuments of Scotland. Reproduced by courtesy of the Trustees of Sir John Soane's Museum: Vol.22, no.284)*

The clock and wind-dial, in the south-east and south-west corner turrets respectively, were made by Vulliamy of London and installed in 1790.

Two smaller-scale but significant public commissions, both monuments, link Robert Adam's name with the circle of Edinburgh's intelligentsia, who in these instances obviously regarded him as the most appropriate artist. The first was a memorial, designed as a pedestal and urn, commemorating the great botanist, Sir Charles Linnaeus, which was erected by Dr John Hope in the Edinburgh Physic Garden, of which he was Regius Keeper, in 1778, 10 years before the founding of the Linnaean Society. Hope was an ardent follower of Linnaeus and lectured to his students on the latter's system of botanical classification. The second commission, to design a monument over the burial place of the philosopher, David Hume, was at the same time an opportunity to pay personal tribute to an old friend.[91] On the site chosen by Hume himself in the Calton burial ground Robert created a dignified cylindrical Roman tomb which, in 1778 when it was erected, had the appearance of clinging to the edge of the Calton hillside overlooking the eastern end of the Nor' Loch, a dramatic topographical setting for this reminder of one of Scotland's immortals. Adam Smith, who had a good view of it from his garden at the foot of the Canongate, is said to have disapproved of the choice of the prominent site as a pompous farewell gesture by his genial and learned friend.

Drawings were prepared for over a dozen Scottish clients in the 1770s in addition to the owners of Culzean, Caldwell, Wedderburn and Mellerstain, some never executed, others partially. They included Aitkenhead House, Renfrewshire, for Thomas Brown; Cavens, Kirkcudbrightshire, for Richard Oswald of Auchincruive, Ardkinglas, Argyllshire, for Sir James Campbell, alterations at Floors, Berwickshire, for the Duke of Roxburghe, and the new wings which Robert schemed for Kilduff House, East Lothian in 1770 for his friend John Home. About the same time he designed the fine town house, now 8 Queen Street and part of the Royal College of Physicians, for Robert Orde, Chief Baron of the Scottish Exchequer, who took the feu in 1769. For some time the only house in that street, its elegant facade with columned doorway and restrained decoration was in contrast to the rather prosaic houses that then lined George Street. The interior preserves a number of features, including the ceilings of the first-floor drawings rooms, some chimneypieces, and the apse and sideboard recess in the dining room, reminders of 'the respected English judge' who, according to Boswell, 'will long be remembered in Scotland where he built an elegant house and lived magnificently'.

Other individual mansions were already appearing around St Andrew Square. They included what is now Number 35, with its attached columns spanning the ground and first floors, crowned with Ionic capitals and fluted frieze running across like a garland under the attic storey, built for the lawyer Andrew Crosbie of Holm in 1769. Lack of documentary evidence prevents firm attribution to Robert Adam but he did make drawings for Crosbie, of which only those for interiors survive;[92] the interior of Number 35 was altered by Archibald Elliot in the early 19th century. Sir William Chambers was probably the architect of

Numbers 23-26 on the north side of the Square and certainly designed the mansion which stands back from the east side, in 1771, for Robert's London client, Sir Laurence Dundas. The ceiling in Sir Laurence's north-east drawing room (now the Board Room of the Royal Bank headquarters which the house has become) is illustrated in George Richardson's *Book of Ceilings*.

As in London, Robert longed to set his mark on the expanding city of Edinburgh, to have a distinctive hand in its transformation. Unfortunately, although his Scottish commissions helped to bring a positive note into the otherwise fraught 1770s, his experience in Edinburgh in the 1780s was to intensify the frustrations and disappointments of that decade.

Robert Adam; now attributed to David Martin, undated. Painted about the height of his reputation, the architect is seen holding a volume (possibly his own *Spalatro* or *Works*), highlighting his interest in and contribution to the literature of his art. *(National Portrait Gallery, London)*

'DISTRESSFULL SITUATIONS'

Whereas the Adams' financial difficulties of the early 1770s reached a crisis, the worst effects of which passed, those of the early 1780s became increasingly serious as time went on. Against this troubled background Robert experienced a drop in creative output even greater than in the 1770s. Then, a certain amount of ongoing English country house work, the creation of a group of fine London mansions and distinctive Scottish castles, government employment in Edinburgh and the publication of *The Works in Architecture* may have helped to blunt the effect of architectural rivalry and adverse criticism.

The later troubles were partly due to the London brothers' failure to learn the lessons of the Adelphi experience. They looked to speculative building and town-planning schemes to revive their fortunes, materially and artistically, and at the same time tried to make good their losses by raising money quickly through ill-considered business ventures. One of these was their bid for a monopoly on the use of stucco (a composition resembling stone) of which they bought the patents of two inventors, David Wark of Haddington and a Swiss clergyman, John Liardet, agreeing to give the latter a share of the profits. 'Adams cement', as it was called, was used by them in an attempt to corner the market for the manufacture of fashionable Adam-style ornaments, they themselves also using it on the facades of their speculatively-built housing and other buildings. In 1778, two years after they had obtained an act of parliament making them sole manufacturers of Liardet's stucco, they sued an architect, John Johnson, for infringement of their rights and Lord Mansfield pronounced in their favour only after a long and tedious court case. They themselves were sued in turn when the stucco failed to reach the accepted standard and fell off, the most damaging case being that raised by Lord Stanhope, and they also quarrelled with the over-sanguine Liardet who refused to accept the decreasing returns from their agreement on the use of the stucco.

A much greater loss was the failure in 1780 of the Battersea and Sandend Company, a saltpetre manufactory and associated barrel-making works, which they set up in partnership with a man whom James became acquainted with, who turned out to be a rogue and absconded with the funds. A more respectable and potentially lucrative operation would have been the contract with the Ordnance Board, gained for them by John's son William who was then treasurer of the Board, which had to be turned down for want of capital. By the mid-1780s William Adam and Company was on the brink of bankruptcy, although the partial nature of the surviving financial papers makes it impossible to have a clear picture of the situation.93 From 1784 onwards the deficit remained at over £30,000. The London brothers owed about £25,000 to John himself and large sums to others who had lent them money in their troubles, from their client the Earl of Findlater (to whom they sent chimneypieces for Cullen without charge in part-repayment) to their collaborator, Joseph Rose the plasterer. On top of all this the development-company's lack of funds began to make inroads into the profits of the architectural practice which had hitherto been kept separate and which before the American war had accumulated over £20,000.

The brothers' different attitudes to their predicament, its origins and remedies, caused an unprecedented and tragic break in Adam family relations. John, ever realistic and unable to withdraw from his partnership in the ill-fated family business, advocated a determined effort to pay off debts and reduce the bank-interest without indulging in any more financial gambles. Yet, while he declared that 'following fantoms had been their ruin' and urged them to stick to 'the plain road of their business', he himself may have hoped for better things from William Adam and Company at the beginning. David Hume seems to have thought so, for in sympathising with the family in the 1772 bank-crash he remarked,

> *'People's compassion I see was exhausted for John, in his last calamity [Fairholm's failure] and everybody asks why he incurred any more hazards. But his friendship for his brothers is an apology; though I believe he had a projecting turn of his own'.*

After all, the Adams had been brought up, as the children of a successful father, to think big and keep several irons in the fire; it was one thing, however, to be an enterprising Scot at home and another to take risks, with only the resources of one's profession, in the 'more extensive' and competitive scene of London. For John all this was supposed to have ended with the 1774 lottery, 'by which we were all reckoned to be licked whole again'.

He was particularly bitter that the turn of events and the unlikelihood of his ever being repaid by his brothers caused him to advertise the Blair estate for sale a second time and, when it still did not sell, to find himself a fairly modest house in Edinburgh. He felt betrayed that 'the Adelphi', as he referred to them in letters to his son, had invested in the Battersea and Sandend business without his consent, although he was their partner and creditor. When it failed he lost all patience:

> *'I lament that so much money has been allow'd to be sunk both to ourselves and others, by a villanous imposter, who surely might have been found out sooner'.*

He believed he could put his finger on one reason for the disaster;

'I never knew a transaction of Jamie's where he did not blunder about the Conditions in the Writings, as he trusts to other people's attorneys [agents] without examining ... We had many instances of this in the Adelphi affairs'.[94]

James, while as Robert's architectural partner he often acted as the client's contact with the practice, was less reliable in business affairs and inclined to take his lead from others, a trait he admitted to when about to join Robert in the early 1760s. As the number of architectural commissions declined in the 1780s he took to living part of the time at the small country house which he had acquired in Hertfordshire and developed an interest in agricultural improvement; perhaps the model of a threshing machine which found its way from the attics into the early 19th century Adam sale may have been a relic of his interest in farming. In 1789 he published a book entitled *Practical Essays on Agriculture*, largely a synthesis of others' writings, which took John by surprise when he saw it advertised in a newspaper; 'Can this be our James?', he asked his son William, 'If so, in the name of all that is good, where has he got this Knowledge?'. It is a pity that with time on his hands James did not publish some of his earlier essays on architecture; some of the excitement seems to have gone out of the art for him in later life. William, the practical businessman by training and nominal head of the development-company, was charged with keeping the Company's books, organising its trading activities and the supply of building materials and sending John regular abstracts of the Company's increasingly-depressing financial state. It was he who in the 1780s conducted the London end of what John afterwards referred to as 'that unmanly and unfeeling correspondence' most of which, mercifully perhaps, has not survived.

John Adam near the end of his life. Paste medallion by James Tassie, 1791. *(Trustees of the National Galleries of Scotland)*

Robert's preoccupation, first and last, was that of a creative artist in the most public and permanent of all the arts, his most compelling motive the desire for self-expression. Yet, the family's precarious position on the brink of bankruptcy meant that he had to be the main breadwinner. Like his father, however, he had a casual attitude to money; John deplored his 'foolish expression of indifference' to the collapse of the Battersea and Sandend Company and complained of his reluctance to check the accounts, although he does seem to have been more assiduous where the accounts of his personal commissions were concerned. He probably took the view that the business side was William's responsibility, his was to 'invent'. It was with William, whom Robert took to Edinburgh with him in 1786 during his battle with the South Bridge Trustees, that John mainly had discussions about their affairs, 'For Robert gave very little attendance'. In a draft letter to William afterwards summarising their discussions but marked 'not sent', John gave expression to his most bitter feelings. In spite of their otherwise 'temperate conversations' about what should be done to weather the threat of bankruptcy and enable John to provide for his family, he had been hurt that

> *'when talking of my affairs and the situation I was brought into, Robert never opened his mouth; But you regretted it saying it was indeed very hard, but you had all lost your fortunes'.*

Nothing can detract from the tragedy of John's circumstances, since Fairholm's bankruptcy increasingly dragged into a situation from which he could not escape. At the same time, Robert's attitude must surely be seen against the background of one of the greatest disappointments of his life, 'an opportunity that does not occur once in a century', the failure of the Trustees to accept in full his grand design for the South Bridge development. Frustrated and angry as the great opportunity to transform this part of the city slipped through his fingers he apparently had little sympathy left over for his older brother. This, coupled with the failure of so many other schemes, real financial worries and a measure of withdrawal

Drawing of the east-facing fronts of the buildings for the west side of the South Bridge scheme, Edinburgh, from the College at the south end (left of picture) to Hunter Square behind the Tron Kirk at the north end (right, shaded), 1785. It shows the colonnaded fronts of the houses and the fine arch planned for the Cowgate, the one feature removed and the other modified in execution. *(Royal Commission on the Ancient and Historical Monuments of Scotland. Reproduced by courtesy of the Trustees of Sir John Soane's Museum, London: Vol.34, no.3)*

by James from what had been the field of their mutual interest, may have thrown Robert in upon himself. It is significant that he should have turned in these years of disappointment to his perennial private interest of painting, creating hundreds of romantic landscapes in ink-wash and watercolour which, although set in the picturesque tradition of the late-18th century, capture his own enthusiasms for classical and gothic, heroic structures and atmospheric landscape. Imaginary though these compositions are, they are linked in the artist's repertoire to those real castles which he was then building in the Scottish countryside.[95]

John Clerk of Eldin, in his notes for a projected biography of his brother-in-law, associated Robert's concentration on landscape painting with the immediately post-Adelphi years, the stress of which broke his health seriously enough to warrant a visit to the curative bathing at Margate. A design in pencil and ink for stables for the Duke of Roxburghe's London house, dating from 1776 and marked '27-29 August Margate, Robert Adam', may be a relic of a working holiday; 'Mr Adam', Clerk remarked, 'never for a moment could be idle'. He also states that in the fraught year 1786 Robert became so ill that he disposed of the collection of landscape paintings to his three sisters, 'on an impression that he should die at the age of 58' and 'to secure a property to them in case their future should suffer by his affairs'. 'You are not ignorant', William reminded his nephew on one occasion, 'of the influence that distressfull Situations have upon Bob's constitution and how much they render him incapable of business'.

Relations between John and Robert were made more embarrassing in 1785-6 by the affair of the South Bridge which brought Robert to Edinburgh more often and made his activities the talk of John's circle of acquaintances, gentlemen and tradesmen, and eventually in the newspaper columns. The aim of Sir James Hunter-Blair, self-made banker, former MP and Lord Provost of Edinburgh, in identifying himself with a great civic undertaking which would be of benefit and convenience to the citizens (without undue expense), was completely at odds with that of Robert Adam who saw the construction of the road-link between Old Edinburgh and its southern suburbs as the opportunity to create a magnificent

piece of classical town-planning, leading to other developments, which would bring fame to the city.

His plan seems larger-than-life in the context of the run-down relic of even Hunter-Blair's Bridge as constructed, let alone the medieval network of wynds and piecemeal 18th century building it was intended to replace. It must be seen as part of the total transformation which he envisaged and delineated in the various drawings which he made in and soon after 1785; the great processional route into the city from the south, with the dome of the Register House (on which work resumed that year) the focal point of the vista. The straight line of this route would have been relieved at the southern end by an elegant crescent facing the University (already mooted), which almost had the character of a forecourt filled with the kind of activities proper to an educated community (concert hall, bookshop, academic residences), and at the northern extremity the great sweep of terraced houses on the natural line of Leith Street, like a flourish after the official statement of the Register House. Added to this were the archways, a triumphal element that always appealed to Robert, one over the Cowgate beneath the new Bridge, where a work-a-day version was actually built, and the other designed to link the east end of Princes Street with the Calton Hill, a natural site for castle-like buildings, where a bridge designed by Archibald Elliot was built in 1815. The South Bridge houses themselves were to have columns rising to first floor height, supporting balconies from which a view might be had of the length of the street, turning the footpath into a sheltered promenade. The Lord Provost's utilitarian priorities were epitomised in his remark that Robert's design for the Cowgate arch was a needless expense since it would only be seen by carters.

The ground of the conflict between the architect and the Trustees as represented by the Lord Provost was at best a misunderstanding, at worst a betrayal of trust. It appears from Robert's letters that he assumed that he had been commissioned to make out plans for an elaboration of the original civic scheme as a result of the detailed discussions which he had had with the Lord Provost in 1785 while the latter was in London about the necessary legislation; Hunter-Blair declined to take this view. There is more than a suspicion that, having seen the architect's general ideas, he was determined to hand the thing over to a local builder to execute as cheaply as possible. The speed with which he got the work underway just before Robert's plans were laid before the Trustees lends support to this theory. The plans having been submitted in August 1785, Robert visited Edinburgh in order to furnish himself with details of the site. A delay in acknowledgement of his designs and, above all, his first-hand assessment of the likely 'mean and bad effect' of the Cowgate arch then being built by Laing, the contractor, infuriated Robert who saw the character of his whole scheme being ruined if he was not immediately given control of the execution. On 30 December he wrote to the Lord Provost, as angry as it is possible to be on paper:

'Will your Lordship forgive me for saying what I really feel on this Subject? That I can suppose this Building so ill managed, and so unskilfully put together, that in place of ornamental and meeting with admiration from the Public, it

may become as ugly and as deformed a piece of Work as ever disgraced a great City. For these reasons I feel myself most exceedingly anxious to have this business put on some proper footing, especially as my name stands at present connected with it and that the World in general think your Lordship is following my plan'.[96]

In an effort to obtain official appointment he proposed to make new plans according to his own revised measurements on the site, to reduce his surveyor's fee, and to modify the design for the house-fronts, having found a method of 'rendering the great Street equally magnificent without Columns, which have been such bugbears to many of the Inhabitants'.

The Lord Provost replied on 8 February 1786, virtually terminating Robert's involvement. On behalf of the Trustees he asked for the bill for Robert's plans and trouble hitherto:

'And as they are conscious that the System which they now find themselves under the Necessity of adopting is not an Object for your Attention or for the incurring of the Expence of an Overseer from London they do not wish you to be at more trouble until it is known whether the plan of a new College can be carried into Execution'.

Never one to admit defeat, Robert fought back throughout 1786. Ignoring the Lord Provost's dismissal, he replied to his letter in March suggesting further improvements to the scheme and rejecting the idea of taking 'some House in the New Town as a model and repeating that through the whole length of the new street' as tedious and just as undesirable as leaving the builders to determine the design of the individual houses. In April, when Sir James Hunter-Blair went to London about the new Act of parliament, Robert and William arranged meetings of London-based Trustees and a number of their own friends at which the new Adam plans were greatly admired, which had the desired effect of isolating the recalcitrant Lord Provost. William almost gleefully reported an incident at one of those meetings to his nephew, young John Clerk, who was orchestrating the efforts of the Adam lobby in Edinburgh:

'The Plan Bob produced today was much admired as indeed it highly merited as I think it prettyer and Grander than the former one with the Columns.

The Provost produced a drawing of Mr Elder's shop as the one they were to follow – Bob immediately said he gave him the Gripes, at which he [the Provost] was greatly offended. Bob put it off with a Joke and the Duke of Buccleugh also turn'd it into a joke by saying that they would make him their Lord Treasury, but Mr Adam must be their judge of Taste'.[97]

The humiliation could have done Robert's cause no good with Hunter-Blair. Nevertheless, it was decided that Robert and William should go to Edinburgh where their objections to the work in execution would be examined before a full meeting. 'You must know that Robert has been kicking up a wonderfull dust in London about his not being imploy'd to conduct the New Bridge', John Adam wrote to his son-in-law, Thomas Kennedy of Dunure, 'which has occasion'd his being sent down to make enquiries, Computations, etc, etc, And William (forsooth) must accompany him ...'. John, one of the major proprietors whose property was subject to compulsory purchase along the line of the new bridge, settled amenably for the figure offered him; not only was he always averse to haggling but to dispute with the Trustees would have made it look as if he identified with his estranged brother over the Bridge business. Robert's representations and 'Observations' and plans were put forward at an unusually friendly meeting, perhaps due to the fact that Sir William Forbes took the chair for the absent Lord Provost, but the Trustees' Report on their submissions was contested by the Adams who complained of obstruction to their practical investigations.

By the summer of 1786 a compromise had been reached about Robert's suggested widening of the Street but by then a damaging battle was going on in the newspapers in which the conventions of anonymity were thrown to the winds, one writer being the young John Clerk who was later to make his name on the judicial bench. By the late autumn the Adams had given in and in March 1787 presented the Trustees with an enormous bill for £1,228 11s for drawings and attendance. It was never paid in full; Robert received £500 in August 1787 and had to settle for a further £400 in November 1789 on the eve of the founding of the new College which was to become a much greater monument to his talents. Nevertheless, the outlines of his plan for the South Bridge had been adopted: the straight street-line, the square behind the Tron Kirk, Blair Street leading back to the Cowgate and the unified treatment (however pale an imitation in the execution) of the house-fronts which he had intended. It was a pity that the rejection of their more modelled frontages raised high over a grand arch deprived any upward-glancing carters in the Cowgate of their glimpse of a slice of the Adelphi transported to Edinburgh.

In 1787 a compromise was also reached with John over the tangled family finances by which the London brothers agreed to pay the English creditors (if and when they could) and John those in Scotland. 'The Adelphi' refused, however, to repay John out of their future earnings. William, in communicating their feelings on the subject, drew a comparison between John's prospects (as the writer saw them), with his remaining property, his shares in the thriving Carron Company and the brilliant career (with its anticipated emoluments) that clearly lay ahead of his son William, and the situation of himself, Robert and James,

'who have not a shilling in the world but have a deficiency above £5,400 to make up ... and all this together with the expense of living to arise out of a precarious business supported entirely on borrowed money and depending upon the health of delicate and worn out constitutions.

He reminded John of how much the building recession of the American War years had affected their attempts to make good, even diminishing the anticipated success of *The Works in Architecture.*

John shrank from 'kicking up a wonderful dust' in public as Robert was prepared to do but his sense of the proprieties had led him to visit Robert at the

Drysdales' home in August 1785 when the plans for the South Bridge were first presented;

'I thought it would look odd in the eyes of Mankind not to see him, as there did not use to be ceremony between us [he told his son]; but if he does not return my call he shall have no further visits from me. I was asked to dine with him at the Provost's today where Dr Drysdale, J Clerk etc were to be but I declined because I am determined not to appear as an Appendage'.[98]

To the end John persisted in the belief that his brothers' aims had been

'nothing more than the expectation of amazing Gains and anticipating the use of them, by which they have brought themselves and me into this dreadful situation',[99]

an understandable, if simplistic, explanation which his son William endorsed when he came to sum up his uncles' careers in the family history which he wrote for his own grandchildren.

Something positive, however, has to be said on behalf of the chief protagonists. Even at his most bitter John could not entirely suppress the instinctive loyalty that had so characterised the 'wonderfully loving' Adam family and drew back from establishing a Trust for his own affairs lest it drive his brothers and sisters into bankruptcy, when 'they must go to the streets'. 'Bad as things have been', he confessed, 'I could not bear that'. Robert, for all his ambition and stubborn refusal to publicly admit his part in what had happened, was sufficiently sensitive to suffer physically and psychologically as a result of the situation. More importantly, with his inherent resilience, he was able to pick himself up and face the renewed challenge of the last few unexpectedly creative years of his life.

Design for the east front of houses proposed to be built on Leith Street, Edinburgh, on ground from which the rents were due to the Register House Trustees, 1785. Among those taking property in the development, whose names appear on the drawing, were James Salisbury, clerk of works at the Register House, and the architect, Robert Burn. The houses, which were to have first floor balconies above shops like those proposed for the South Bridge, were not built. *(SRO, Register House Plans, 6080)*

'GREAT ENCOURAGEMENT
in the LINE
of his PROFESSION'

Although it is true that Robert's late Scottish commissions date mostly from 1789 onwards that is not to say that they represent merely a last-minute flurry of activity. Those dating from about 1780 to 1788, although fewer in number, included important and innovative work the designs for which, whether built or not, show this to have been a creative period.

It included the castles of Oxenfoord, Midlothian (1780-2), Dalquharran, Ayrshire (1781-5, although internal work was still going on in 1790), and the most exciting phase of Culzean. With Sunnyside, built (1785-6) for the Midlothian laird Sir Patrick Inglis, there began a line of comparatively simple yet often ingeniously-planned villas in the 18th century tradition that had earlier interested John Adam. There were country houses for gentlemen who, although they might have interests in the south, intended to live much at home, such as Jerviston near Holytown in Lanarkshire, built (1782-4) for James Cannison and Kirkdale, Kircudbrightshire, built (1787-8) for Sir Samuel Hannay, from a long-established Galloway family. More prestigious was work at Yester, East Lothian, which had undergone various alterations since William Adam had modified James Smith's original house in the 1730s, where Robert, having made designs for alterations to the saloon by John in 1761, transformed the great room in 1789, by giving it 'three fine broad and lofty windows', and building an elegant new north facade, the existing drawing for which is believed to be by James Adam.[100]

The geographical pattern of the commissions expanded, especially in the West of Scotland where, in addition to Culzean and Dalquharran, there were designs for the famous 'New Brig' (1786) and Town Steeple (1785) at Ayr, and two houses which in the end were not built, Barholm, Kirkcudbrightshire, designed (c.1787-9) for John McCulloch and Glasserton, Wigtownshire (1787) for Admiral the Hon Keith Stewart. Hopeful clients approached Robert during his annual visits to Scotland. In April 1786, in the midst of meetings about the South Bridge, he had to convey his apologies to William Forbes of Callendar, through James Nisbet the plasterer, for being unable to go to Callendar House near Falkirk, to give his opinion on plans.

'[Mr Adam] is extremely sorry it is impossible for Him to Wait on You at Callendar House – but as His business will detain him here till Friday – He thinks if You were in Town with the plans He would be very Glade to Spend a Couple of hours with You and would be happy to point out anything that would be of Service'.[101]

Nothing seems to have come of this attempt to involve him in the modernisation of Callendar House.

On 20 October 1789, the day on which he attended a meeting in Edinburgh to discuss the forthcoming foundation of his new College buildings he wrote to Thomas Kennedy,

'I have had so many applications about plans for houses from all parts of the Countery this trip, that I have been obliged to send for one of my Clerks from London to assist two others I imploy here, so that I hope I shall be no loser by remaining at Edinburgh till the foundation stone is laid the 16th of November'.[102]

The entrance front of the University, Edinburgh, founded 1789; Robert Adam's most monumental design in Scotland. It is shown here in 1829 during Playfair's completion of the building. A large dome (larger than that originally intended) was added by Rowand Anderson in 1887. *(Thomas Shepherd, 'Modern Athens')*

Elevation of a proposed crescent on the east side of the South Bridge, Edinburgh, facing the new College, designed by Robert Adam in 1791: containing (centre) Concert Room, tea-rooms, retiring rooms, etc; (south) bookseller's or stationer's, rooms for the Highland Society; (north) Coffee Room or Eating House; (in the intermediate spaces) ten shops with kitchens and bedrooms for the shopkeepers. The Crescent would have been an extremely civilised complex had it been built. *(Royal Commission on the Ancient and Historical Monuments of Scotland. Reproduced by courtesy of the Trustees of Sir John Soane's Museum, London: Vol.34, no.12)*

With the founding of the new College in 1789, perhaps because of the publicity it gave Robert's work among landed and professional men who were encouraged to subscribe to it, he received an increasing number of requests for designs for a range of buildings. There were villas, like Newliston, West Lothian, built (1789-91) for Thomas Hog, merchant, banker and enthusiastic farmer, which is still lived in by his descendants, and Rosebank, near Cambuslang on the Clyde, for John Dunlop, Glasgow merchant, for which the unexecuted drawings are dated 1789-92. Late classical mansions included Balbardie, near Bathgate, West Lothian, designed for Alexander Marjoribanks and his family of 19 children, about which Robert was in touch with the client in 1791 although the existing

Remodelled north front of Yester House, East Lothian, c.1789; drawing attributed to James Adam. *(Royal Commission on the Ancient and Historical Monuments of Scotland)*

Country villa: Newliston, West Lothian, designed by Robert Adam for Thomas Hog and built 1789-90. A much grander transformation of the old house had been designed by William Adam for the Earl of Stair, the previous owner, in the early 1720s but not adopted. *(Royal Commission on the Ancient and Historical Monuments of Scotland)*

drawings are dated 1792-3; Gosford, East Lothian, built for the 7th Earl of Wemyss from 1790 onwards, elements in its design going back to the architect's study of the Emperor Diocletian's palace at Spalatro; the Earl of Lauderdale's 'snug place where he means to live mostly when he comes to Scotland', built 1790-92; and the interior of Archerfield House, East Lothian, where work was done in 1790-91 for William Nisbet of Dirleton. Balbardie has gone, Gosford, although much altered, is still owned by the client's family, the Earl of Lauderdale's house still stands, minus its former glory, in Dunbar High Street and Archerfield is an empty shell.

A number of castles, the designs for some unexecuted or completed after Robert's death, were in progress from 1789-92. Of these the grandest is Dalquharran, Ayrshire, (completed about 1790) for his niece, John's daughter Jean, and her husband Thomas Kennedy of Dunure, where plans to transform the ancient castle by the River Girvan as had been done at Culzean were abandoned and the new castle with its great central tower was built more fittingly on rising ground. As at Culzean the staircase formed a spectacular central feature, in this case round instead of oval. The castle, after being derelict for many years, awaits restoration. Pitfour in Perthshire, attributed to Robert Adam on stylistic grounds, was still under construction in the 1790s; its appearance was considerably altered in the 1820s and in more recent times it has both benefited from restoration and suffered from fire. Designs for a castle on an ambitious scale were drawn up in 1790 for Col. William Fullarton, Ayrshire, but only the stables appear to have been built to the original plans. Seton, the most mature of the late castles, and happily still lived in, was built on the site of the old palace which was demolished to provide stone for the new castle. Having come to an agreement with the owner, Alexander Mackenzie, lawyer and son of a Peeblesshire laird, in the summer of 1789 Robert engrossed the detailed building contract of 12 November in a personal notebook.[103] A dramatic composition of tall, variously-shaped towers, the front of the house rears above the entrance archway to an enclosed courtyard. Mauldslie Castle, Lanarkshire, was built after Robert's death for the 5th Earl of Hyndford, although the design was made and the house was probably founded in 1791 during the architect's last visit to Scotland. Like other late Adam castles it has a number of features that derive from the Scottish castle tradition, such as the round towers with cap roofs that have been compared to those at Holyroodhouse, the crow-stepped gables, the bartizans on the angles of the parapet and the coat-of-arms on the battlement. Stobs, in Roxburghshire, the very last Adam castle, still stands although, having been built without the architect's supervision, its appearance diverges somewhat from the drawings.

On 3 October 1789 John reported to his son,

'I met Robert one day upon the Street, when turning a Corner. We were both surpriz'd but behaved with Civility to each other, as one Gentleman should do to another. The short Conversation we had, turn'd upon the Visits he had paid, and was to pay to different people in this Countrey, in the way of his profes-

sion; And he said a good deal about His plan of the College. He ended by saying He was going to East Lothian, to Lord Wemyss's and Mr Nisbet of Dirleton's for two days, And if I would come when he return'd He would show me everything. Upon which I made a bow and walked off. This was a week ago, and I hear he is not yet set out for London, which I think has an odd look, as if His imployment in London was totally gone, so that He must hang on here, like a man in dependance'.[104]

John's surprise at Robert's hanging about in Edinburgh almost suggests that he knew little about the unofficial discussions and string-pulling which must have

Entrance Front of Dalquharran Castle, Ayrshire. This early engraving shows the less dramatic elevation of the building which stands on rising ground above the river Girvan.

Robert Adam's niece, Jean, daughter of John Adam and wife of Thomas Kennedy of Dunure for whom Dalquharran was built. Although enjoying their new castle the Kennedys had their portraits painted against a backdrop of the family's ancient keep at Dunure. Portrait by Sir Henry Raeburn. *(Trustees of the National Galleries of Scotland)*

preceded the announcement by Principal Robertson to the Senatus of the University on 19 October, to the effect that a few days previously the Lord Provost had informed him and several of the Professors that

'The Town Council had come to the Resolution to have the foundation stone laid of a new building for the University, designed by Mr Robert Adam, Architect, on the 16th of next month'.

As with the Register House, Robert would have been aware for some time of the long-felt need for a new University building and of the various attempts to raise support and money for the project from government and town council. These had included his cousin the Principal's *Memorial relating to the University of Edinburgh* of 1768, and *A Letter to the Right Honourable Henry Dundas* of 1785 in which the author, believed to be Professor James Gregory, referred to the elevation of the College which Robert had included in his drawing for the South Bridge scheme and hoped that the University's well-wishers might be 'favoured with a complete plan of a new College from the same masterly hand'.[105]

No documentation has so far come to light about precisely how or when Robert was officially commissioned to design the College but he could write to Thomas Kennedy of Dunure on 3 October, the very day on which he invited John to come and see his plans, that 'What chiefly brought me down this Autumn was to Show a plan I made for a new College and brought with me from London'. At that point the plan had been seen by a number of people, for he went on,

'I have hitherto found every body, Ministerial & Antiministerial, High and Low, rich and poor & all the professors pleased with the design & eager to have it carried into execution under my direction. They seem also most willing to subscribe for that purpose ... What I wish is to get the foundation stone laid & the building sett agoing. I have very little doubt of the Success of it But till it is begun no body will Subscribe or take any concern about it. We are assured of having a very liberal aid from Government next Year. But private exertion will be the best Spur to public aid As it will show that we do not entirely depend on their Assistance for our University'.[106]

Briefing on the practical arrangements and varied accommodation required must have pre-dated the drawing up of the plans and could only have come from his cousin, Principal Robertson, and his academic colleagues.

Even before the laying of the foundation stone on 16 November Robert made certain that his role as Surveyor, with the right to employ contractors according to their prices, was made absolutely clear. This was not done without some opposition, although, as Robert remarked to Principal Robertson, he had anticipated the direction from which it came: John Gray, clerk to the newly-appointed College Trustees, who had also been clerk to those for the South Bridge. Gray's quibble about the inclusion of a clause in the Subscription Paper establishing Robert's right to the direction of the undertaking was thought to have been prompted by Henry Dundas, and for a time influenced the new Provost, James Stirling. Rather than relinquish his Surveyorship, which he regarded as 'the very best way of preventing all jealousies', Robert threatened that he would be

> '*under the necessity of declining all further concern in this business, & after spending so much time & pains, have the mortification of returning immediately to London with the disagreeable reflection that my plan has not had the effect to accelerate this great & important Work, which I had so much at heart*'.

His threat won him the first round and on 18 November, two days after the foundation ceremony, the Trustees at their first meeting endorsed his demand for full authority over the construction for a fee of 5 per cent of the building costs, awarding John Paterson, clerk of works, a salary of £100 a year, and the right to exercise full authority in the architect's absence.

Another obstructionist to Robert's exercise of his powers was Alexander Reid, Deacon of the Masons' Incorporation, who complained that if the architect was to make contracts and set prices what was to be the role of the Trustees? By the autumn of 1790 Reid, as new Convener of the Trades of Edinburgh became a Trustee himself but with the help of influential friends on that body and his nephew by marriage, Andrew Dalzel, Secretary to the Senatus, and the support on the spot of John Paterson, Robert overcame the objections of the Town and Trade lobby. Reid's quarrel was a personal one against the architect and his clerk of works. Initially failing to gain the important building contract, he was nevertheless given a second chance to tender lower prices which he did, only to go back on his word once his materials had been unloaded on the site. John Paterson rejected Reid's plea for an increase in prices and asked him to leave, after which the contract was given to his competitor James Crichton. As work at last went ahead in earnest Robert wrote congratulating his man on the spot, hoping that

> '*the Trustees will treat with indignation any Private Machination or any Vexatious objections that may fall from one of their body who I am informed is so hostile to me that he has openly avowed that he would delight in any thing that would embarass the execution of this great work*'.

The trouble cannot simply be attributed to personal animosity, or to the autocratic manner of the architect from the metropolis and his impatience with local vested interests. John Adam, with his experience of the building world, must have known better than simply to say that he foresaw Robert's loss of his Edinburgh employment 'as I hear the same degree of Vanity, not to say insolence continues'. The problem lay at the roots of the Edinburgh building tradition in which a number of master-masons and builders were in the habit of undertaking all necessary work for a client and the most enterprising of them went in for the speculative building of squares and streets on their own initiative. They were capable at a practical level and with the help of builders' manuals that took some account of current styles of putting up what the client wanted. The necessary joinery, plumber's work and plasterwork could be agreed with fellow-craftsmen. These builders, of whom Reid was one, resented what they saw as the intrusion of the man who had designed the building – the architect – into their territory of construction, deciding the minutae of the building processes and, by fixing acceptable prices for workmanship, taking decisions for the employer, the client.

Robert Adam was fighting not only for himself but for his profession, which had barely attained recognition at the end of the 18th century, and it was largely in Scotland where his public commissions occurred that he did so. If justice was to be done to his own design and, at the same time, the hard-won subscription money was to be well-spent, he must be seen to be in overall charge. Professional architect though he was he could not be accused of a lack of practical knowledge of the building trades – even although he had once said to Lord Kames that ideas should come first, then the practicalities. If, in Lord Hopetoun's words, he was 'well-advanced' by the age of twenty he must have been particularly receptive to the transmitted experience of his father who had been a working mason. His own practical training was acquired on the building-site of Fort George where, as contractors under Colonel Skinner, the designer, the young Adams had made out plans while the grit and brick-dust drifted through the windows. In writing to clients Robert was as authoritative on the materials and methods of construction as on the visual effect of his designs. Nor was his mind always allowed to dwell on 'the true, the simple and the grand';

> 'Shall I make the Octagon pier in the Center of the Doctor's Store room of Broached, or Droved Ashler or Ruble work', John Paterson wrote to him from the College where the citizens exclaimed at the extravagance of the professors' accommodation and the latter complained that it was not commodious enough, 'will the walls be Better of Ashler or plaister; if of Ashler what kind shall I make them of; the passage that leads to the Common priveys I think was agreed to be Droved Ashlar, may the Circular passage that leads to the Same and to the room for exercise be of Ashlar also and what kind –'.

The peculiar needs of the Professor of Anatomy, Dr Munro, required special facilities in the only part of the College's inner buildings begun in Robert Adam's lifetime;

> 'I told Dr Munro this day since receiving your letter what you say about the pit he wishes to have – he is certain that burying the remains of his Subjects is the Best way but he Still wishes to have a pit 15 or 20 feet deep for sundrie purposes he wants – he insisted on me so much that I said I would write you again – ...'.[107]

Undoubtedly 'grand' is the east (entrance) front of the College which was sufficiently advanced during Robert's lifetime to enable him to judge the effect: 'something handsome' indeed. The triumphal arch with its soaring columns (which the Provost and citizens had feared would be too much for the new South Bridge during transit from the quarry) provides a heroic threshold to the academic precincts. Also impressive in its stark way is the tall domed space which is entered next, which evokes the great vaults of those Roman ruins among which Robert himself had wandered as a wide-eyed student of antiquity. The inner quadrangle, modified in the early 19th century by William Playfair who was born the year the College was founded, has an enclosed feel suited to its purpose as a place of study. The design of the new (now 'Old') College, although it proved too ambitious for the available funds for it to be completed as he intended, was the most monumental of all Robert's designs for public buildings, surely one of the grandest visual reminders of a former student in his *alma mater*.

The need to spend much more time in Scotland in the late 1780s affected Robert's working and domestic arrangements. There was nothing off-stage about the supporting role of his London sisters and Edinburgh relatives whose personal letters over the years carry many allusions to the architectural and business activities of their brothers, although there is an unfortunate paucity of correspondence for the 1760s and early 1770s.

John Clerk of Eldin, husband of Susannah Adam, who had become familiar with the family while a young merchant in the Luckenbooths, was more like a fourth brother than a brother-in-law to Robert with whom he shared artistic interests, sketching together and corresponding about Clerk's particular interests in etching and the aquatint process. Robert colour-washed the collection of etchings which his brother-in-law presented to the King and helped to sell his book on *Naval Tactics* among friends in London. Their tastes in topographical drawing were similar and John Clerk once reminded Peggy Adam that he had copied many of Robert's drawings. In later years he sometimes acted as a contact with the latter's clients and sent the architect reports on the progress of work. He kept an eye on the goings-on at the College and had at least one 'altercation' with John Paterson, about the best way to erect the columns on the east front.

On 2 June 1788 he reported on work at Sunnyside, Midlothian, and looked forward to Robert's annual visit: 'we will get into our new house [? in Princes Street] time enough to give Brother Robert the reception we would wish for I am happy to hear he is to be our Guest'. Robert arrived in mid-September suffering from a bout of influenza caught on the journey, but once he had recovered he set out for Culzean and meetings with the Ayr magistrates about the Bridge.

'We thought it right', Susannah wrote to Peggy in London, *'that Mr Clerk should go with him as it is a very long journey to Colean & will probably take as much time to accomplish as Bob took to come from London ... if the weather continue good they will both be much the better of the Expedition'.*[108]

Before leaving Edinburgh for the West Robert received an anxiously awaited letter from London where Jenny was seriously ill. She died towards the end of the year, having been housekeeper-in-chief of the London household for 30 years. In January 1789 Robert apologised to Lord Findlater for the delay in finishing the design for the latter's proposed new castle on the Banffshire coast: 'the long distress in our Family and at last the loss of my oldest sister, was a great barr to application in business; One of my clerks also left me, which is a loss I find great difficulty in supplying'. By the autumn of that year, however, after he and John Clerk had visited Cullen, he was inclined to blame the client's own indecision for the delay. He wrote on 20 October to his client at Dalquharran, Thomas Kennedy: 'I have made a new edition of a plan for Lord Findlater but whither he will ever begin to build I do not know, If a new edition could be made of himself I would be more able to answer your question'.[109] In spite of John Adam's estrangement from Robert, his daughter Jean Kennedy and her husband remained her uncle's appreciative clients. Work on the interior of Dalquharran was well in hand when Robert wrote to the clerk of works, Hugh Cairncross, on 23 April 1790, listing those working drawings which he was about to dispatch on the mail coach and giving instructions about the library:

'in the section of the library I have drawn composition ornaments in the pilasters & frize of bookcases that can be put in at any future time if Mr Kennedy should incline to have them, or left plain if he chuses them so. On the tops of the bookcases I have also placed busts & figures which I suppose to be cast in plaister, the pannells above are supposed to be painted on paper or cloth & pasted or hung regularly round the room. Opposite the chimney I think a library table should be placed with a glass frame over it, which would be both ornamental & convenient'.[110]

In February 1791, in replying to a letter from his son-in-law John Adam assured him, 'It gives us also great pleasure that your house turns out so comfortable & so much to your mind. We sincerely wish you all health & long life to enjoy it'.[111] It must also have given the architect pleasure to have a satisfied family client.

As Robert became based in Edinburgh over the summer and autumn each year his remaining unmarried sisters, Peggy and Betty, took to accompanying him, or making their own way north, to spend some weeks in Scotland. To begin with Peggy hesitated;

'You and Mrs Drysdale have both been wishing us to come down with Bob if he goes this summer', she wrote to Susannah Clerk in 1789 '... we think there are insurmountable objections arising from the unsufferable depravity of the servants in this place, and the things that are left in this house are not like what other people leave behind them because the Books and drawings are like the Stock in trade and are at the same time very perishable ...'.[112]

Posterity owes it to the Adam women for their care of their brothers' drawings in later years. As late as 1796, after Robert and James were both dead, Mary Drysdale packed up those drawings left in the Edinburgh office and sent them to London, where her sister Peggy had mixed feelings about the task of sorting them out, because as Mary explained,

'... I did not consider them as at all safe in this place ... and I was quite unhappy at their being at the mercy of anybody that chused to go into Cairncrosses house when he was out of it and break open the box and take out any drawings they pleased. I always had a dread of that fellow Patterson playing some mischief and was glad when I got them away'.[113]

Mary and her husband, the Rev Dr John Drysdale of the Tron Kirk, were, with the Clerks of Eldin, strongly partisan on the London household's side in the family quarrel with John, and Mary in particular was a watchful guardian of Robert's reputation. On one occasion she rapped the knuckles of Sir William Forbes the banker who tried to get hold of an Adam design on the cheap. Having been passed a note from Forbes to John Clerk of Eldin in which the banker asked for a sight of *The Works in Architecture* 'as he thinks he recollects that there is among them a Section of Lord Mansfield's Library at Kenwood from which he may get some useful hint ...', Mary sent a brusque reply to her sister Susannah, whom she may have felt was less likely to give in to the great man than her husband:

> '*My dear Susy – I have the Plans but it strikes me that I have no right to give away Robies Plans without his leave asked and given, and I really think that is a Proper answer to Sir William, he is an impudent Raskall or he could not have asked such a thing of Mr Clerk ... The Book is my Property and I will not give it out of my hands without leave. Mr Clerk may say he does not know anyone that has it. Eight or ten pound will get Sir Wm a Plan of his own. Mr Clerk might tell him it would be far more genteel to have a thing made for himself than to pilfer from Lord Mansfield*'.[114]

In a very different mood she tried to bring about a reconciliation between her estranged brothers.

> '*My dear Johnie*', she wrote on 23 August 1789, '*I have intended these two days past but have always been prevented by something or other to let you know that your Brother Robie is here, And I would fain offer my advice to you to come & call for him. I know nothing could be more agreeable to him than to see you and I cannot help thinking it much more agreable to both parties to be on tollerable terms than the situation you are in at present. I am perhaps using too much freedom but the desire I have to bring you together has made me venture on what you may reckon impertinent*'.[115]

John, thanking her for 'your wish that it should be otherways', declined the invitation; regarding himself as the injured party he felt it was not his place to make advances. A verbal invitation from Robert when they met accidently on the street and a later written offer to let John see the College plans were also declined. There is evidence of business contacts between the brothers in the spring and summer of 1791, when John explained the circumstances of Robert's contest with the troublesome College tradesmen to McLeod of Geanies, and constituent of his son William, MP for Ross-shire, who wanted a plasterwork contract for a local tradesman; 'My brother has promised Mr Gilchrist's employment', he wrote in July while Robert was in Edinburgh, 'He is to give me timely notice when the work will begin'.[116] The episode may have led to a measure of personal communication.

One result of the increased work-load and acrimonious atmosphere of the late 1780s which worried the family was the deterioration of Robert's health.

> '*We have been uneasy about the complaint in his stommach which has been so long a tiresome complaint to him*', Peggy wrote in the autumn of 1789 during the run-up to the founding of the College, '*but in his last letter he said he was going to dine at the Principal's which looks as if he were pretty well again,*

but nothing in the world is worse for him than Feasts ... I dare say there will be a Prodigious crowd to witness the Procession on the 16th of next month, but it is a bad time of the year and if it rains it will be a disagreeable business'. '[Bob] suffers the pain when he wants his dinner long, and the Beef tea that Mary prescribed it is almost impossible to administer to him here for he is never to be catched at a proper time'.[117]

By December 1789 John Adam could report to his son on Robert's movements:

'I understand now he intends spending a great portion of his time in this place, and that Mrs Drysdale is to take a larger house ... as the Sisters, Draftsmen, etc are also to come down'.[118]

Mary, who had been widowed in 1788, moved in 1790 from the area known as Society (near the west end of the present Chambers Street), where Robert on his own admission had made 'a sad confusion in her house' with his draughts-men, to 14 Nicolson Street which was also near work in progress at the College. Her home became his Scottish workbase during the last two years of his life.

In 1790 he was in Scotland from mid-May to early October. Before leaving London, according to his sister Peggy's letters, he was 'looked to by many people as the person that ought to be employed in the New Opera House ... it would be a pity to neglect it as it may turn out profitable and at any rate is a fine subject for genius'. She also reported how he had attended one of the Prince of Wales's levées, where 'he kissed his hand, The Prince spoke a good while to him very civily'.[119] There were a number of developments north of the Border that summer and autumn. In addition to work at the College, progress was made on

Seton Castle, East Lothian, the most striking of Robert Adam's late houses in the castle-style. The massing of the variously-shaped towers and the curve of the wall enclosing the courtyard, entered by a central arch-way (not shown), gives the maximum sense of movement to the whole composition. *(Royal Commission on the Ancient and Historical Monuments of Scotland)*

Lord Lauderdale's house at Dunbar, details of which Robert wrote carefully into his notebook which also contains details of work to be done at Cluny Castle, Perthshire.[120] Of Seton Castle John Paterson reported on 15 March:

> '*I am obliged to go ... tomorrow with Mr McKinzie, when I was there last I found there was 50 feet less ground to Build on than you was made to believe by the plan of the ground you got from him ...*'.

On 26 April, however, he was able to say that he had again gone to the site with the owner who was anxious to have his house founded:

> '*[I] ... measured the ground before him and pointed out the Spot where the great Tower Should Stand ... all of which he was well pleased with and I set of and laid the found stone before I left the place ...*'.[121]

In September and October Robert made out a detailed statement of the many drawings done for Archerfield House for William Nisbet of Dirleton. That for the Rotunda dated 'Edinburgh 4 September 1790' was copied to 'Mr Coney ... to do all ornaments and any necessary mouldings'. Coney was also employed

that year at Culzean; according to Robert's instructions to Hugh Cairncross this was in spite of his drinking as Lord Cassillis expressed a dislike of new people.[122] An ambitious scheme which developed in Robert's mind in 1790, although the drawings date from the following year, was that for the accommodation of the Advocate's Library which he came to envisage as a combined scheme for the Library and the Court of Session. The advocates' approach to him, repeating an earlier request for his advice of 1769, was initially made by the Faculty Treasurer Allan MacConochie through John Paterson. Sadly, Robert's plans for a group of public buildings lying to the west of the Parliament Hall and associated with a plan for opening up West Bridge Street (south of the Lawnmarket) came to nothing in the end.

Before the end of 1790, again thanks to the resourceful Paterson, he had been approached for a design for the proposed Charlotte Square, for which his drawings are also dated the following year. While Paterson was talking to the Provost at the College in October, they were joined by James Stirling's predecessor, ex-Provost Elder, who showed the clerk of works the plan for the Square at the West end of the Town drawn by James Nisbet the plasterer.

'I confess I hardly looked at it, but as the provost paid you several very handsome compliments in the course of this conversation, I took the liberty of saying it was misfortunate that there had been so little attention paid to the Building in the New Town, had a front been drawn by you of the New Town it would have had a very different effect, they both agreed with me, & says Mr Stirling I am determined to have Mr Adams opinion of this Square if it is built in my administration ...'.[123]

By late November the Provost confessed to Paterson that opposition to Robert's being consulted had arisen in the Council, 'they having nothing to say but you would draw the Town into a great expence both for your designs and the execution of them'. He hoped for Elder's support, however. The indignant clerk of works remarked that 'a good workman was worthy of his hire', commended Nisbet's public spirit but stated that Mr Adam would undoubtedly make more of the opportunity to design the new Square. The plans for Charlotte Square, executed after his death, were to be his most influential contribution to the New Town of Edinburgh.

In 1791 he left London on 15 May for what turned out to be his longest visit to Scotland, lasting until early January 1792.[124] His account book of daily expenses and memoranda for that year has survived, containing references to 30 commissions and over 60 individuals, exclusive of relatives, with whom he was in contact. A number of entries are particularly valuable in showing that he had a personal connection with some of those late commissions which were not built until after his death. He crossed the Border into Eskdale on 21 May, breakfasted at Langholm, took luncheon at the famous Mosspaul Inn and arrived at Edinburgh on the evening of Sunday 22 May, having dined at Eldin on the way with John and Susannah Clerk.

From early summer until mid-July he travelled mainly in the Lothians but also as far as Mauldslie in Lanarkshire, which claimed his attention several times that summer and for which he noted the time-scale of payments at the front of his notebook, a total of £4,855 to be paid by June 1793. Several clients paid him for plans and surveying, including Lord Lauderdale, 50 guineas, and Alexander Marjoribanks of Balbardie whom he drove out to see on 30 May. He took a lease of Alexander Keith of Ravelston's quarry of Wellcraig, for £34 a quarter, and visited Hopetoun, with its early associations, to collect Lord Hopetoun's subscription to the College, £100 for 5 years. A three-day visit to East Lothian on 9-11 June included the site where the Earl of Wemyss's great classical mansion of Gosford was to be founded on 4 August, Dunbar to inspect progress on Lord Lauderdale's house, and Seton, where plasterwork was in progress and where he dined with his client Alexander Mackenzie on Saturday 11 June before returning to Edinburgh that night. The next two weeks were spent in the city except for a social visit on 25 June to the Whim near Penicuik, where as guest of James Montgomerie, Chief Baron of Exchequer, he stayed overnight, losing 6 shillings at cards and catching 'a feverish cold'. On 2 July, the day before his 63rd birthday, he set out for Mauldslie, to which he later dispatched his assistant Andrew Cairns, under whose superintendence the house was to be completed 5 years later.

Balbardie House, West Lothian; vignette on a plan of the Balbardie estate, 1824. *(SRO Register House Plans, 20593)*

His itinerary from mid-July until the end of September included two journeys to the west of Scotland where his practice was then beginning to open up. Important public commissions in Glasgow, to which was to be added work for some private clients, had followed a meeting between the enterprising John Paterson and the Stirling brothers in March 1791. There are few details of Robert's first visit to Glasgow that summer but he spent about a week in the West during which he may have presented his plans of the new Trades Hall, for which his existing designs were accepted on 23 August in preference to those of two other architects. While in the West he visited William MacDowall of Garthland's Castle Semple estate in Renfrewshire, for which a Culzean-type reconstruction of an old castle was planned but not adopted, and stayed with a family friend, Robert Bogle of Daldowie, who at one time had been called in to advise on the tangled Adam finances. Once more based in Edinburgh he met Allan Maconochie on 20 August, probably for discussions on his proposed plans for a new Advocates' Library, and on 23 August drove out to Thomas Hog's villa of Newliston and then on to Balbardie. On 24 August he was made a burgess and guild-brother of Edinburgh *gratis*.

His second visit to the West, of which there are more details, began when he set off for Mauldslie on 10 September, calling later at Jerviston, where he had

Mauldslie Castle, Lanarkshire, probably founded in 1791 while the architect was in Scotland *(Drawn by J Fleming, engraved by Joseph Swan)*

designed the house for James Cannison nine years earlier, and Daldowie. The week beginning 13 September was a busy one spent in and around Glasgow where he lodged at the Tontine hotel in the Trongate, his bill for lodgings, service in the Coffee Room and newspapers also includes 2s for a plan of the city. On Wednesday 14 September he met with the Assembly Rooms Committee, for whom drawings were prepared in 1791 and early in 1792. After business he drove out to Carmyle with the prominent Glasgow merchant, John Dunlop, calling on the way at Rosebank on the Clyde near Cambuslang which Dunlop had recently acquired. Robert made plans for its transformation into a classical villa early in 1792 but, like many late projects, it remained unexecuted and the unaltered house was sold to the cotton manufacturer, David Dale, in 1801. On 15 September he met other two committees, that for the new Trades Hall, already founded on 9 September, who 'agreed unanimously to give me Sole direction and surveying and paid on Account thereof £52 10s', and that for the projected Infirmary, the founding of which was to be attended by James Adam two months after Robert's death. The account book gives no indication of what stage his business with the Infirmary committee had reached.

During the next three days he made several journeys out of the city; on 16 September he visited Castle Semple and next day Walkinshaw, near Barrhead, the drawings for which show it to have been one of his most cleverly planned late houses, designed in the Edinburgh office that year for Dayhort MacDowall, son of the client at Castle Semple. On the way to Castle Semple itself he had called 'with Mr Burn at Linthouse, Mr Sprouls'. Plans for Linthouse were prepared at Edinburgh in December, James Sproull paying him £21 'in full of Plans' on 4 January. Like Walkinshaw it has been demolished. On 18 September he dined at Drumpellier with Andrew Stirling, to whose influence he owed his public commissions in Glasgow and left the city on the following day to spend two nights at Blair Drummond with George Drummond, son of his old friend Lord Kames. Various existing designs for a Culzean-type castle there presumably relate to his visit at this time.

Varied business awaited his return from the West at the end of September and by mid-November Professor Andrew Dalzel, wrote to a friend:

'*Mr Robert Adam has remained in Scotland longer than usual this season, having got great encouragement in the line of his profession. He is to carry on some public building in Glasgow ... and he is carrying on several private buildings in different parts of the country*'.[125]

Robert's business prospects, although they made for much labour and travelling, must have created an optimistic mood in the Edinburgh family circle that winter. On his third visit to Glasgow, from 8-13 November, he took with him his sisters Peggy and Betty who had joined him in Edinburgh in September; 'spent on the road with B[etty] and Peggy, 14s'. During the winter the family made arrangements to view the Register House, now functioning although incomplete; Peggy Adam's note to her sister Susannah runs, 'if this day would suit you and Mr Clerk and the rest of the family to go and see the Register Office we would meet you there half an hour after 12 o'clock ...'. It is likely that being in the town Robert himself conducted the family round the building which had given his career its first major public break through in Edinburgh twenty years earlier.

Occasional memoranda show him spending his evenings with Edinburgh friends: 'a chair to Professor [Dugald] Stewart's', 'to 3 suppers at the Oyster cellar', 'lost at cards at Mr Convin's, 5s', 'to the Play with Mrs Robertson', when possibly his cousin, Principal Robertson, kept his alledged promise to his father never to enter a theatre. On Christmas Eve Robert was in William Creech's bookshop, that haunt of notables, where he bought a copy of Good's *The Measurer and Tradesman's Assistant*. His few personal expenses include, in addition to gloves, buckles and the predictable pomatum and hair-powder, that sign of ageing, a pair of 'seeing glasses'. There are several charitable payments to an 'Alexander Adam' and 2s 6d to 'the letter man's Christmas Box'. The entry, 'to the Musical Glasses, 7s 6d', may indicate attendance at or a purchase of this popular form of public and private music-making. On Christmas Day he gave his Clerk nieces ten guineas and at New Year made his sister Mary Drysdale a present of four silver salt-cellars, made by the goldsmith, William Robertson and costing 7 guineas. He paid the taxes on Mary's house and a statement of their account, settled on Hogmanay 1791, is written into his memorandum book. John Robertson, the clerk, who later had an architectural career of his own, received a pair of boots with his weekly guinea at the New Year. The draughtsman Joseph Bowes signed an agreement with his master on 2 January to work for £25 a year, receiving 5 guineas 'as a present for past attendance'. Bowes later went to America where he referred to his experience in the Adam office when advertising for employment in the Philadelphia newspaper.

The Edinburgh Bridewell, founded on St Andrew's Day, 1791, Robert Adam attending the ceremony. Two other Adam buildings are visible; the Dome of the Register House (right) and the David Hume tomb on Calton Hill. *(Drawn by A Carse, engraved by R Scott, c.1805)*

The most notable professional event towards the end of the year was the founding of the Bridewell on Calton Hill on 30 November. This important penitentiary building had been designed by Robert in evolutionary stages that year as he corresponded with Jeremy Bentham, whose *Panopticon; or the Inspection House* (London, 1791) had influenced his competition-winning design. Bentham's brother later claimed that Robert Adam had not sufficiently acknowledged his debt, but by the time Bentham and he began to correspond in late May Robert claimed to be already working on the 'principle of invisible inspection', which was central to the Panopticon, whereby the layout of the building enabled the jailor to have a complete view of the entire interior. The Bridewell was completed in 1795 but was demolished in 1884.[126]

An unfortunate circumstance in an otherwise successful season was a quarrel with the clerk of works, John Paterson. In December Robert was obliged to tell the College Trustees that he was no longer able to employ him and that his place had been taken by Hugh Cairncross. So far no information has come to light on what went wrong but it was apparently serious enough for the Adams to raise a court action early in the year. Robert's death may have caused it to be abandoned.[127]

On 6 January 1792 Robert left Edinburgh, John Robertson travelling with him in the post-chaise and his manservant, John Hindsley, on horseback. Next day he dined at Stobs with the Elliots and proceeding on his journey reached London on Thursday 11 January when his note, 'to keeping my chaise and going to Kenwood', indicates a visit to Lord Mansfield. The payment on 3 February of his subscription of a guinea to 'the Liberal Society', a society which met on

Early 19th century view of Robert Adam's Glasgow Infirmary, founded after his death. *(Drawn by J Knox, engraved by Joseph Swan)*

Sundays to hear philosophical lectures, shows him picking up the threads of his life in London. The following weeks were not without frustration. Constant travelling and a considerable work-load during 8 months in Scotland had taken their toll of a man who had driven himself all his working life and whose health had long been giving cause for concern. On top of this he was confined to the house with a leg-injury sustained soon after his return to London. He seems nevertheless to have been able to supervise the work of his draughtsmen on plans for several commissions, including some Glasgow buildings, Stobs and Balbardie.

The Glasgow Assembly Rooms business caused some unpleasantness in the form of the committee's reply to his enquiry as to whether or not they wished an estimate; 'they did not' and 'would let him know if they have any occasion for him ...', which provoked an outburst from Peggy at 'this sort of reply to their own countryman, the first in his profession ...'. One cheering piece of Glasgow business was the £40 received from Mr John Mair for designs for two houses in George Square, now vanished with the rest of the Square's early buildings. The drawings are dated 22 and Robert noted the payment on 25 February. This is the latest entry in his memorandum book.

On Friday 2 March Robert suffered a severe and unexpected stomach haemorrhage at his home in Albemarle Street and died early on Saturday afternoon. Having written to Mrs Drysdale on Friday night describing the attack William broke the news of his brother's death in a letter to Susannah Clerk late on Saturday:

'... he Sleeped very composedly the first part of the night but all at once the vein open'd again about 4 o'clock this morning when he threw up a vast quantity of blood that weakened him ... he however revived again but ... only strug-

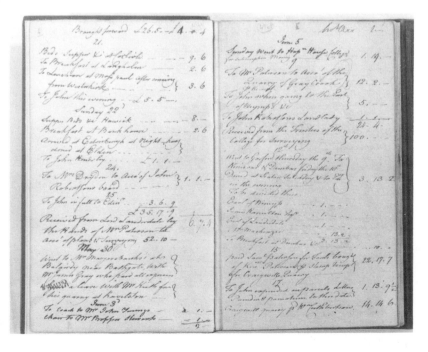

Pages in Robert Adam's personal memorandum and account book which he used on his last visit to Scotland in 1791. Six commissions are mentioned on these pages. *(SRO, Clerk of Penicuik Muniments: GD18/4968)*

gled for life in very great Pain till 2 oClock when he became quiete and went off very easily'.[128]

In a postscript, written because in their distress the family forgot to post the letter, William authorised Mary Drysdale 'as Bob would have wished' to spend £200 on mournings for the Clerk and Drysdale families, including Andrew and Anne Dalzel's two children. Their third child, born a month later, was baptised Robert Adam Dalzel.

Robert was buried privately in the south transept of Westminster Abbey on 10 March. The pall-bearers, apart from the Earl of Coventry, were from Scottish families: the Duke of Buccleuch, the Earl of Lauderdale, Viscount Stormont representing Lord Mansfield, Lord Frederick Campbell and Mr William Pulteney.

'*Lady Clerk tells us*', Susannah wrote to William '*that the Consternation when the accounts came to town was General & that nothing else was spoken of and it was look'd upon as a great Publick Calamity, indeed the loss of no Individual that I know cou'd have been so much felt*'.[129]

Principal William Robertson expressed a more personal loss in a letter to Andrew Dalzel on 7 March:

'*You will easily conceive how much I was surprised and afflicted with the melancholy event which you communicated to me last night. I have lived long and much with many of the most distinguished men in my own times, but for genius, worth and for agreeable manners, I know none whom I should rank above the friend we have lost ...*'.[130]

The Adam era which by his efforts Robert had extended in Scotland almost to the end of the century was nearly at an end. James, somewhat reluctantly if family letters are any guide, travelled periodically to Scotland to attend to the late

Principal front for a new design for Rosebank, on the Clyde, for the Glasgow merchant John Dunlop, with whom Robert Adam discussed the commission during a visit to the West of Scotland in 1791. This drawing, dated 1792, was one of several supervised by the architect in the weeks preceding his death in London on 3 March. *(Royal Commission on the Ancient and Historical Monuments of Scotland. Reproduced by courtesy of the Trustees of Sir John Soane's, Museum, London: Vol.30, no.48)*

commissions until his own death in 1794; it seems that as in the early years of his London practice so in his last years in Scotland Robert had been largely alone in realising his ideas.[131] John, whose stewardship of the family fortunes had enabled Robert to take his own way in youth, died only three months after him in June 1792. William survived on, after the inevitable bankruptcy, until 1822. Sales of Robert's and James's fine collection of books, paintings and antiquities in 1818 and 1821, including over 160 volumes from Robert's magnificent library, helped him to survive. In 1822 young Susan Clerk, who had gone to London to keep house for her Aunt Peggy and Uncle William, offered the vast collection of architectural drawings accumulated in over 30 years of practice to the British Museum, without success. Eventually, in 1833, Sir John Soane purchased almost 9000 drawings for £200. They are today part of the collection of works of art and architectural drawings in the Sir John Soane Museum, his house in Lincoln's Inn Fields, London, where they may be consulted by students from all over the world.

Robert himself left his mark on Scotland to which he returned not only to spread his particularly inventive interpretation of classicism but to develop a unique late style of castle-building, which owed a great deal to the buildings and landscape of his native land. The soaring east front of the College of Edinburgh trapped in a narrow street is a reminder at one and the same time of the triumphs and disappointments of his later career, his design for Charlotte Square is his last word over his hesitant civic patrons, for it was the historic catalyst which rescued the New Town of Edinburgh from prosaic provincialism and put it in the international class to which the architect himself belonged, while Culzean demonstrates what 'a picturesque hero' could do with a Scottish upbringing and a classical education.

Robert Adam, 1792; paste medallion by James Tassie based on a death-mask taken by the sculptor, Joseph Nollekens (*Trustees of the National Galleries of Scotland*)

REFERENCES

1. (SRO) Registers of Testaments: CC20/4/16, fos.100v-101 (Alexander Adam, mason d.1698); CC20/4/20, fo.17 (Thomas Adam, mason, d.1748); Register of Deeds, Mack, 61, fo.974 (marriage contract of Charles Adam, mason, and Elizabeth Wishart, dau. of Thomas W. at Mill of Glamis, 1685); Mack, 177/2, fo.122 (Mr Patrick Adam, d.Jamaica, 1747). (General Register Office) OPR288/1, Forfar (Adam baptisms). I am grateful to Dr William Kay for corroborating my conclusions about the probable identities of the brothers of John Adam, senior.

2. (SRO) Broughton and Cally Muniments: GD10/1421/9/412/1.

3. (SRO) Clerk of Penicuik Muniments: GD18/4728/5.

4. Andrew G Fraser, *The Building of Old College* (1989), p.96.

5. (SRO) Exchequer records: E307/4, pp.118-119.

6. (SRO) Marchmont Muniments: GD158/1303/1.

7. *Ibid*, GD158/2507.

8. (SRO) Montrose Muniments: GD220/5/1059.

9. Clerk of Penicuik Muniments: GD18/4727.

10. *Ibid*, GD18/5005.

11. (SRO) Court of Session processes: CS230/42/1.

12. Clerk of Penicuik Muniments: GD18/4981-82; biographical details attributed to John Clerk are taken from this source unless otherwise stated.

13. Blair Adam Muniments: 4/225.

14. (NLS) Milton Papers, MS16665.

15. Montrose Muniments: GD220/5/935/10.

16. *Ibid*, GD220/5/935/9.

17. *Ibid*, GD220/5/935/16

18. Alistair Rowan, 'The Building of Hopetoun', in *Design and Practice in British Architecture, Studies ... presented to Howard Colvin* (1984), 184-209.

19. Clerk of Penicuik Muniments: GD18/4737.

20. *Ibid*, GD18/4783.

21. *Ibid*, GD18/4853.

22. John Fleming, *Robert Adam and his Circle in Edinburgh and Rome* (1962), p.340.

23. Work at Banff Castle, (SRO) Seafield Muniments: GD248/984/4; Castle Grant, *Ibid*, GD248/108. *See also*, James Macaulay, *The Classical Country House in Scotland* (1987), pp.130-2, and p.141 where other SRO sources are cited. Work at Arniston, see Mary Cosh, 'The Adam Family and Arniston', in *Design and Practice in British Architecture*, pp.214-30, and Register House Plans, 5248/5-21.

24. Seafield Muniments: GD248/951/5.

25. (SRO) Ross of Balnagowan Muniments: GD129/7/7/3.

26. (SRO) Campbell of Stonefield Muniments: GD14/99.

27. Clerk of Penicuik Muniments: GD18/4884.

28. British Architectural Library, Drawings Collection, RIBA: Robert Adam's sketchbook, 1749-50, L12/3.

29. John Fleming, *Robert Adam and his Circle*, p. 310.

30. L.T.C. Rolt, *Thomas Telford* (1958), p.9.

31. Clerk of Penicuik Muniments: GD18/4764.

32. *Ibid*, GD18/4775.

33. *Ibid*, GD18/4770.

34. *Ibid*,

35. *Ibid*, GD18/4777.

36. *Ibid*, GD18/4789.

37. *Ibid*, GD18/4796.

38. (and 44)(SRO) Abercairny Muniments: GD24/1/564.

39. Clerk of Penicuik Muniments: GD18/4836

40. Ibid, GD18/4811.

41. Alexander Carlyle, *Autobiography* (1860), pp.358-9; Clerk of Penicuik Muniments: GD18/4848.

42. *Ibid*, GD18/4854.

43. *Ibid*, GD18/4866.

44. See 38, above.

45. Clerk of Penicuik Muniments: GD18/4948.

46. *Ibid*, GD18/4942.

47. *Ibid,* GD18/4884.

48. (SRO) Oswald of Auchincruive Muniments, Letter Book, GD213/54, pp. 27, 39

49. Seafield Muniments: GD248/250/1.

50. W S Craig, *The Royal College of Physicians of Edinburgh*, (1976), pp.73-4; Drawings in the Soane Museum, Volume 28: 37-44; Clerk of Penicuik Muniments: GD18/4853, 4942.

51. W Forbes Gray, 'An Eighteenth Century Riding School', *Book of the Old Edinburgh Club*, Vol.20 (1935), pp.111-59.

52. F C Mears and J Russell, '*The New Town of Edinburgh*', *Book of the Old Edinburgh Club*, Vol.23 (1940), p.8; I R M Mowat 'Urban Development in 18th Century Scotland: John Adam as Town Planner', *Bulletin of the Scottish Georgian Society*, 10 (1983).

53. Innes of Stow Muniments: GD113/3/349; Letter on the loss of the commission, Clerk of Penicuik Muniments, GD18/4876.

54. *Ibid*, GD18/4888.

55. Seafield Muniments: GD248/178/2/10, 11, 13; see also, James Macaulay, *The Classical Country House in Scotland*, pp.132-4.

56. (SRO) Dalhousie Muniments: GD45/18/2245.

57. Drawings for ceilings at Cullen: (SRO) Register House Plans, 2542.

58. Seafield Muniments: GD248/590/3/19/1-2.

59. Alistair Rowan, 'Yester House, East Lothian, III', *Country Life*, 23 August 1973, p.490.

60. Montrose Muniments: GD220/6/1471/21; related drawings in Soane Museum, Volume 43: 16-20.

61. (SRO) Carron Company Records: Letter Book, GD58/6/1/12, pp.191, 378. Discussed in R H Campbell, *The Carron Company* (1961) p.77.

62. Blair Adam Muniments: 4/188.

63. *Ibid*, 4/5.

64. *Ibid*, 4/190.

65. *Ibid*, 4/189.

66. *Ibid*, 4/184.

67. Clerk of Penicuik Muniments: GD18/4866.

68. *Ibid*, GD18/4876.

69. Alistair Rowan, 'After the Adelphi: Forgotten years in the Adam Brothers' Practice', *The Royal Society of Arts Journal*, Vol.CXXII (1974), p.678.

70. Blair Adam Muniments: 4/10.

71. Quoted in James Lees-Milne, *The Age of Adam* (1947), p.31.

72. Fanny Burney (later Mme D'Arblay), *Early Diary and letters*, 1768-78, Vol.1, April 1770.

73. Blair Adam Muniments: 4/10.

74. *Ibid*, 4/229.

75. *Ibid*, 4/3.

76. *Ibid*, 4/184.

77. (NLS) Paterson-Adam Correspondence, MS19992-3; 14 March 1790.

78. Clerk of Penicuik Muniments: GD18/5549/21.

79. (SRO) Biel Muniments: GD6/1644/1-2.

80. Paterson-Adam Correspondence, 13 April 1791.

81. Clerk of Penicuik Muniments: GD18/4966.

82. (SRO) National Register of Archives (Scotland), Survey 104: Haddington Muniments, p.62 (Original at Mellerstain).

83. (SRO) Ailsa Muniments: GD25/9, Boxes 8, 9 and 10 contain papers relating to the building of Culzean Castle.

84. NRA(S) Survey 104, p.62. (Original at Mellerstain).

85. Alistair Rowan, *Designs for Castles and Country Villas* (1985), p.17.

86. *The Caldwell Papers* (Maitland Club, 1885), Vol.2 Part 2, CCLXI; drawings for Caldwell House: Register House Plans, 2549.

87. Register House Plans, 6082/7.

88. Alan A Tait, 'The Register House; The Adam Building', *Scottish Historical Review* (1974), p.115.

89. (SRO) Scottish Record Office Records: 4/43/1.

90. *Ibid*, Trustees' Minute Book, 4/1, pp.42-3.

91. Iain Gordon Brown, 'David Hume's Tomb: A Roman Mausoleum by Robert Adam', *Proceedings of the Society of Antiquaries of Scotland*, Vol.121 (1991).

92. Soane Museum, Volume 29: 120, 127.

93. Blair Adam Muniments, section 4 passim; for discussion of the Adam finances based on this source, see Alistair Rowan, 'After the Adelphi', pp.659-74.

94. Blair Adam Muniments: 4/194.

95. Alan A Tait, 'The Picturesque Drawings of Robert Adam', *Master Drawings*, Vol.9 (1971) pp.161-71; same author, 'Robert Adam and John Clerk of Eldin', *Master Drawings*, Vol.16 No.1 (1978), pp.53-7; same author, catalogues of two exhibitions, '*Robert Adam and Scotland: The Picturesque Drawings*' (Scottish Arts Council, 1972) and *Robert Adam at Home, drawings from the Collection of Blair Adam* (Scottish Arts Council, 1978).

96. Andrew G Fraser, *The Building of Old College*; Chapter 3, 'Robert Adam and the South Bridge Scheme', contains quotations from papers in the National Library of Scotland relating to the scheme. Copies of these papers are to be found in (SRO) Clerk of Penicuik Muniments: GD18/5838. Robert Adam's letter to the Provost, 30 December 1785, GD18/5838/5.

97. *Ibid*, GD18/5838/2.

98. Blair Adam Muniments: 4/213.

99. *Ibid*, 4/199.

100. Robert Adam to Professor Andrew Dalzel about Yester House: (SRO) Yester Muniments: GD28 Supplementary papers, Box 3/3 (photocopy). Drawings

for Yester, 1789, in the Soane Museum, Volume 41: 5-9.

101. (SRO) Forbes of Callander Muniments: GD171 Box 13.

102. Original letter in the National Monuments Record of Scotland; I am grateful to Mr Ian Gow for a copy of this letter and that cited under 106.

103. Clerk of Penicuik Muniments: GD18/4965.

104. Blair Adam Muniments: 4/221.

105. Andrew G Fraser, *The Building of Old College*; Chapter 4, 'The Adam College, 1789-1804', cites many documents from the archives of the University and the City of Edinburgh.

106. See 102, *above*.

107. (NLS) Paterson-Adam Correspondence, 15 March 1790.

108. Clerk of Penicuik Muniments: GD18/5486/16.

109. See 102, *above*.

110. NRA(S) Survey 104, p.62. (Original at Mellerstain)

111. Blair Adam Muniments: 4/229.

112. Clerk of Penicuik Muniments: GD18/4961/15.

113. *Ibid*, GD18/5549/19.

114. *Ibid*, GD18/5553-4

115. Blair Adam Muniments: 4/216.

116. Ibid, 4/206.

117. Clerk of Penicuik Muniments GD18/4961/18, 20.

118. Blair Adam Muniments: 4/216.

119. Clerk of Penicuik Muniments: GD18/4961/22.

120. *Ibid*, GD18/4965.

121. (NLS) Paterson-Adam Correspondence: 15 March and 26 April 1790.

122. (SRO) Dalquharran Muniments: GD27/7/323.

123. (NLS) Paterson-Adam Correspondence: 30 October 1790.

124. For a fuller account, *see* Margaret H B Sanderson, 'Robert Adam's Last Visit to Scotland, 1791', *Architectural History, Journal of the Society of Architectural Historians of Great Britain*, Vol.25 (1982) pp.33-46.

125. Andrew Dalzel, *History of the University of Edinburgh* (1862), Vol.1, p.90. Robert Adam designed a 'cottage ornée' for Dalzel who married his niece, Anne Drysdale: undated drawings in the Soane Museum, Volume 46: 152-4; the plan of a Greek cross may be an allusion to the fact that Dalzel was Professor of Greek at Edinburgh University.

126. Thomas A Markus, 'Buildings for the Sad, the Bad and the Mad in Urban Scotland, 1780-1830', in Thomas A Markus, ed, *Order in Space and Society* (1982), pp.25-114.

127. Clerk of Penicuik Muniments: GD18/4961/37, 39.

128. *Ibid*, GD18/4972.

129. *Ibid*, GD18/4973.

130. Quoted in Andrew Dalzel, *History of the University of Edinburgh*, Vol.1, p.94.

131. Margaret Adam's letter on James having 'lived so much in the country and had not an opportunity of knowing much of what was doing in the architecture part of the business', 28 March 1792, Clerk of Penicuik Muniments: GD18/4961/40. John Clerk of Eldin's comments on James not using his talents latterly, 13 March 1792, *Ibid*, GD18/4974/1.

FURTHER READING
and REFERENCE

ADAM, Robert and James
The Works in Architecture of Robert and James Adam, 1773-78; 1779; 1786; 1822.
Reprint, with Introduction, by Robert Oresko (Academy Editions), 1975. Reprint, with Introduction by Henry Hope Reed (Dover Publications, New York) 1980.

ADAM, William
Vitruvius Scoticus, 1812. Facsimile edition with Introduction by James Simpson (Paul Harris) 1980.

BEARD, Geoffrey
The Work of Robert Adam (John Bartholomew 1978); second edition, Bloomsbury Books, 1987.

BOLTON, Arthur T
The Architecture of Robert and James Adam (1922) 2 vols.

BROWN, Iain Gordon
Building for Books, The Architectural Evolution of the Advocates' Library, 1689-1925 (Aberdeen University Press and The National Library of Scotland) 1989.

BROWN, Iain Gordon
'David Hume's Tomb: A Roman Mausoleum by Robert Adam', *Proceedings of the Society of Antiquaries of Scotland,* vol.121 (1991).

BROWN, Iain Gordon
Monumental Reputation: Robert Adam and the Emperor's Palace (1992).

BROWN, Iain Gordon
'The Resemblance of a Great Genius', Commemorative portraits of Robert Adam', *The Burlington Magazine,* CXX (1978), pp.444-61.

CHERRY, T A and BROWN, I G
Scottish Architects at Home and Abroad (1978).

COLVIN, Howard
A Biographical Dictionary of British Architects 1600-1840 (John Murray 2nd edition) 1978.

DAVIS, Michael C
The Castles and Mansions of Ayrshire (1991); includes all known Adam Works in the County.

DUNBAR, John
The Historical Architecture of Scotland (Batsford) 1966.

FLEMING, John
Robert Adam and his Circle in Edinburgh and Rome (John Murray) 1962.

FLEMING, John
'Robert Adam's Castle Style', *Country Life,* vol.143 (23 and 30 May 1968), pp.1356-59 and 1443-47.

FRASER, Andrew G
The Building of Old College: Adam, Playfair and the University of Edinburgh (Edinburgh University Press) 1989.

FREW John and JONES, David, editors
Aspects of Scottish Classicism: the House and its Formal Setting, 1690-1750, St Andrews Studies in the History of Scottish Architecture and Design (1988).

GIFFORD, John
William Adam, 1689-1748: A Life and Times of Scotland's Universal Architect (Mainstream) 1989.

HARRIS, Eileen
The Furniture of Robert Adam (1963).

HARRIS, John
Sir William Chambers (1970).

KING, David
The Complete Works of Robert and James Adam (1991).

LEES-MILNE, James
The Age of Adam (1947).

LINDSAY, Ian and COSH, Mary
Inveraray and the Dukes of Argyll (1973).

MACAULAY, James
The Classical Country House in Scotland, 1660-1800 (Faber) 1987.

MACAULAY, James
The Gothic Revival, 1745-1845 (1975) Especially Chapters 6, 'Robert Adam's Northern Castles' and 9, 'The Scottish Contemporaries of Robert Adam'.

McCORMICK, Thomas J
Charles-Louis Clérisseau (The Architectural History Foundation, Inc, New York) 1990.

ROWAN, Alistair
'After the Adelphi: Forgotten Years in the Adam Brothers'

Practice', *The Royal Society of Arts Journal*, vol.CXXII (September 1974), pp.659-710: text of the Bossom Lectures (1974).

ROWAN, Alistair
Designs for Castles and Country Villas by Robert and James Adam (Phaidon) 1985.

ROWAN, Alistair
'Paxton House, Berwickshire', *Country Life*, vol.142 (17, 24 and 31 August 1967), pp.364-67, 422-25, 470-73.

ROWAN, Alistair
'Robert Adam's Last Castles', *Country Life*, vol.156 (22 August 1974), pp.494-98.

ROWAN, Alistair
'Sunnyside and Rosebank: suburban villas by the Adam brothers'. *A A files, Annals of the Architectural Association School of Architecture* no.4 (July 1983), pp.29-39.

ROWAN, Alistair
'Wedderburn Castle, Berwickshire', *Country Life*, vol.156 (8 August 1974), pp.354-57.

SANDERSON, Margaret H B
'Robert Adam's last visit to Scotland, 1791' *Architectural History, Journal of the Society of Architectural Historians of Great Britain*, vol.25 (1982) pp.33-46.

SKINNER, Basil
Scots in Italy in the 18th Century (National Galleries of Scotland, 1966).

STILLMAN, Damie
The Decorative Work of Robert Adam (1966).

SUMMERSON, John
Architecture in Britain: 1530-1830 (The Pelican History of Art, 6th edition) 1977: especially Chapter 26, 'William Chambers and Robert Adam'.

TAIT, Alan A
Robert Adam and Scotland: the Picturesque Drawings (1972): Scottish Arts Council Exhibition.

TAIT, Alan A
Robert Adam at Home: drawings from the Collection at Blair Adam (1978); Scottish Arts Council and RIBA Exhibitions catalogue.

TAIT, Alan A
'The Picturesque Drawings of Robert Adam', *Master Drawings*, vol. 9 (1971), pp.161-71.

TAIT, Alan A
'The Sale of Robert Adam's Drawings', *The Burlington Magazine*, no.120 (July 1978) pp.451-54.

Various AUTHORS
Design and Practice in British Architecture, Studies in Architectural History presented to Howard Colvin (The Society of Architectural Historians of Great Britain) 1984.

Various AUTHORS
William Adam, Architectural Heritage I (The Architectural Heritage Society of Scotland) 1990.

YOUNGSON, A J
The Making of Classical Edinburgh, 1750-1840 (1966).

SCOTTISH RECORD OFFICE SOURCES

An extensive Source List of Documents in the Scottish Record Office relating to Architecture may be consulted in the Historical Search Room, General Register House, Princes Street. The Historical and the West Search Room (West Register House, Charlotte Square, Edinburgh) are open, Monday-Friday, 09.00-16.45, closed certain public holidays. Readers' tickets are issued on personal application and production of proof of identity. Staff will advise on the location of individual sources; drawings and plans are held at West Register House, private archives (family papers) are held at the General Register House.

A full List of Scottish Record Office publications and other items for sale is available on request. All enquiries to:

Scottish Record Office HM General Register House Edinburgh EH1 3YY

031 556 6585

HMSO publications are available from:

HMSO Bookshops
71 Lothian Road, Edinburgh, EH3 9AZ   031-228 4181
49 High Holborn, London, WC1V 6HB   071-873 0011 (counter service only)
258 Broad Street, Birmingham, B1 2HE   021-643 3740
Southey House, 33 Wine Street, Bristol, BS1 2BQ   (0272) 264306
9-21 Princess Street, Manchester, M60 8AS   061-834 7201
80 Chichester Street, Belfast, BT1 4JY   (0232) 238451

HMSO Publications Centre
(Mail and telephone orders only)
PO Box 276, London, SW8 5DT
Telephone orders 071-873 9090
General enquiries 071-873 0011
(queuing system in operation for both numbers)

HMSO's Accredited Agents
(see Yellow Pages)

and through good booksellers